Imagin Action

Using Drama in the Classroom — No Matter What You Teach

by

bobbi kidder

Cottonwood Press, Inc.
305 West Magnolia, Suite 398
Fort Collins, Colorado 80521

ISBN 1-877673-26-9

To Misha, my sister/daughter

Once I passed a torch to you;
now we pass it between us.

Acknowledgments

Thank you:

- to my husband, Ed, always looking out for me

- to my aunt/soul mate, Noots, a keystone in so many lives, certainly in mine

- to Cheri and the Cottonwood Press staff for their patience and clarity

- to Suz for reminding me to get started, for helping me start

- to Lutz and the Rogue Community College family for saying yes to my ideas so often

- to Brooke and the Arts Council of Southern Oregon for all the opportunities, for the network of artists whose work inspires me

- to the Teen Theatre Family and the Alive Together and Stand Tall Troupes, whose excellence and energy supported my creative efforts

- to Lauren, Lisa, Melissa, Dick, Donna, Loraine, Laura, Lorna, Bec, Jeri, Russie, Pat, Barbara, Mary G., Lefty, Belle, D.J., Susan, Lori, Esther, Richard, Nancy and other friends and colleagues whose participation and encouragement has meant so much

- to my middle and elementary school friends

- to my middle and elementary school teacher friends, especially Ruth, Julia, Pat, Coyote Woman, Jack, Nancy and Martha

- to my father and mother

- to the angels

Table of Contents

(continued)

Introduction

So, what *is ImaginACTION?*

ImaginACTION is a book about active learning. With active learning, nobody hides in the back row. All students are up and moving (not necessarily all at once!) — participating, demonstrating, thinking on their feet, using their imaginations, working together and working toward a goal.

"But they're already active enough!" you may be thinking.

Don't worry. *ImaginACTION* helps them *focus* their energy in a positive way. It uses drama to unleash imaginations and make ideas come alive.

Best of all, active learning helps students learn some important life skills:

- They learn to communicate more clearly.

- They grow in courage and confidence.

- They learn to focus their energies in a positive way.

- They learn to take risks.

- They learn to work more effectively in teams.

What is my role, as teacher?

As teacher, you facilitate, encourage, cheerlead, direct, coach — all the things you already do.

Okay. But what if I can't act?

Because *ImaginACTION* activities borrow from the field of drama, non-drama teachers are sometimes nervous about trying them. "I'm not an actor!" they say. "I don't know a thing about drama."

There's nothing to worry about. The easy-to-grab activities in this book will ease you into active learning, if you are new to the concept. You, as the facilitator, can go at a pace you feel comfortable with.

And you will be in good company. In addition to its use by innovative educators, active learning is being used more and more for team building by businesses, civic groups and other organizations. It helps people of all ages communicate more clearly and effectively.

Okay. I'm starting to understand. But I'm still a little worried. Am I going to have to bark like a dog?

You're not the first person to ask that question. The truth is that, no, you don't have to bark like a dog . . . unless, of course, that's what you feel like doing.

And neither do your students. The purpose of *ImaginACTION* is to help students become more confident in expressing their ideas. Asking them to jump way out of their comfort zone would certainly defeat that purpose. *ImaginACTION* activities allow students to gain confidence gradually, growing as they take small risks. No one — including you — has to do anything he or she really doesn't want to do.

Will I feel silly leading these activities?

The first time you try anything new, you are likely to feel a bit uneasy or awkward. That's okay. Feeling uneasy shouldn't force you back into your seat. Your comfort level will increase as you experiment more and more with active learning. Go slowly.

New skills take time. You need to remember that, and to help your students remember it too. Look over the activities in *ImaginACTION* and imagine them succeeding in your classroom. Start small. Choose an activity and try it with your class. As you think about it later, ask this question: What did I like about how this activity went today, and what would I do differently next time?

Then try the activity again. And again. Adapt it to your needs. Change this and that. Add a few frills. After you have repeated it several times, it will become yours. Repetition is essential to becoming comfortable as an active learning facilitator.

So — am I going to wind up with creativity, or just plain chaos in my classroom?

There is a difference between creativity and chaos. Creative group work feels good. Students talk and laugh together as they make decisions. There is a feeling of positive energy. Chaotic group work does *not* feel good. It is unkind, often physical, and always unproductive. It is important to recognize the difference.

ImaginACTION activities are designed to generate creativity, not chaos. There will be noise sometimes, but it should be a productive kind of noise. You will learn strategies for bringing a group back to order and for helping students stay on task.

As you and your students become more and more comfortable with active learning, group work will become more and more focused. Students will be active, interested and excited about what is going on in their classroom.

Active learning may be a good idea, but it's just another new thing to try. I have too much stress in my life already.

Good news: Active learning actually releases stress. It's a lot of fun and productive at the same time — for both you and your students.

It's also easy. You don't have to prepare a lecture, create an overhead transparency or type up a worksheet. With almost no preparation, you can start *ImaginACTION* in your classroom tomorrow.

Just select an activity. Read about it, and imagine yourself leading the activity in your class. Then give it a try. Students like active learning. *You* will like what they learn from it.

Tell me again — why am I doing this?

Active learning helps students build important life skills:

- **Effective communication.** The activities in *ImaginACTION* help students learn to communicate their ideas effectively. They learn that body language, tone of voice, and facial expression are even more important than words in communicating a clear message.

  They also learn to think on their feet. People who can think on their feet increase their ability to get any job they want, and to be effective at whatever they do.

- **Teamwork.** *ImaginACTION* activities help students learn to work effectively in teams. Students develop the ability to stand up for their ideas and, at the same time, to really listen to other people. They learn that working with others and accomplishing a goal together can be both enjoyable and productive.

- **Risk taking.** One of our biggest fears as human beings is speaking or performing in front of others. One reason appears universal: "I'm afraid I'll make a fool of myself."

  ImaginACTION helps students get past worrying about making a fool of themselves. As they take risks about expressing their ideas, they learn that feeling foolish isn't so bad. Nobody wants to feel foolish all the time, but shifting our perceptions a little can give "I feel foolish" less power over our lives.

- **Focus.** *ImaginACTION* activities help students learn to focus — in other words, to prepare mentally to give a task their full attention. When they focus, they are able to concentrate, to think more clearly and to understand better.

Sprinkle *ImaginACTION* activities into your curriculum throughout the year. You will enjoy the positive results!

A Few Basics

"A Few Basics" includes information about getting started with *ImaginACTION* activities. It includes suggestions about classroom management, room arrangement, teamwork and more — all to help ensure the success of active learning in the classroom.

You Are Here

"You are here." That's what maps say when they want to help you get oriented. You can see where you are and where you want to go.

That's what this chapter is all about — getting oriented. The following basics will help you get started with active learning activities in your classroom.

Audience. Before you start *ImaginACTION* activities, teach your students a simple classroom management procedure. Explain:

*Let me introduce you to a special word we are going to use whenever we do **ImaginACTION** activities. The word is "AUDIENCE."*

Whenever you hear me say "AUDIENCE," you have two choices. You can either fall silent immediately or repeat the word "AUDIENCE" once, softly, and then fall silent.

I'll use the word "AUDIENCE" whenever I need to be heard. You can do the same.

The "AUDIENCE" approach is a respectful way to get students' attention. It works well and helps build a sense of group responsibility during active learning. The whole group is responsible for knowing the signal and responding appropriately.

The Space. When you do *ImaginACTION* activities with a group, you need somewhere to do them. That somewhere might be at the front of the classroom one day. On another day, it might be the center of the room, with all the desks moved to the sides. On another day, it might be 30 individual places around the room, one for each student.

You might want to adopt an idea from the American Conservatory Theatre (ACT) in San Francisco. In its code of conduct, ACT refers to "The Space." The Space is any designated area where acting takes place. It might be a stage. It might be somewhere else. What is important is that it is special and set apart with special rules that apply to anyone entering The Space. In a school setting, many of the rules will be rules that also apply to the whole school:

- Get rid of gum.

- Leave food and drink outside.

- Treat others with respect.

However, students need to understand that there are additional rules that have to do with supporting each other in creative activities. The basic rules:

- Pay attention to fellow students and the instructor.

- Be supportive. (Boost people up instead of tearing them down. Resist the temptation to "direct" others.)

- Give your best and participate fully. (Put away other homework, notes from friends, etc.)

- Avoid talking and whispering, as fellow students might perceive such side talk as negative criticism.

- Accept criticism as a chance to improve. Use what you can and "lose" the rest. Defensiveness just gets in your way.

You and your students can come up with other rules together, if you like.

Your comfort level. If you are new to active learning, start small. Try an activity. (The activities in the chapter called "Easy Beginnings" are good ones to try first.)

Then try the activity again. Change what didn't work well, or explain it a different way. Repetition is very important, for each time you repeat an activity, you will become more comfortable. As your comfort level increases, so will the comfort level of your students.

Side coaching. Viola Spolin coined the term "side coaching" in her book, *Improvisation for the Theater* (Northwestern University Press, 1983). It refers to that gentle yet insistent "voice on the side" that instructors of drama activities use when they want students to think more deeply, to stay on task or to find a way to wrap it up. By talking to the actors from the sidelines, the instructor can help actors develop a scene further, look at a subject in a different way or change directions.

When you side coach, it is important to say what you want, not what you don't want. For example, "Find a way to wrap it up now" is preferred over "Don't let this thing go on too long now."

The A-word. Before students begin some activities, it may be a good idea to talk about the word *appropriate*. What do you expect in terms of appropriate subject matter and behavior when students are performing? Be clear with the students, just as you expect them to be clear in their presentations. If *appropriate* means "no profanity," say so. For some teachers, it might mean "nothing that would get us in trouble if the president of the school board dropped in," or "anything that could be rated G, like a family movie." For other groups, *appropriate* might mean "nothing that is cruel or humiliating to anyone." You set the standards appropriate for your group.

"But I was going to do that!" Students often worry that someone will "take" their idea. Just say:

*It's all right if someone uses an idea you were going to use. Go ahead and present **your** version. If it's very similar, add something specific. Make it as clear as you can. You will bring your own flare to the scene.*

Creating the Right Space

Moving furniture is one of the most fundamental jobs in getting started with *ImaginACTION* activities. Students need a designated place to "perform," and that often involves rearranging the classroom.

The move can involve random shoving, crowding and chaos. Or it can be transformed into an effective activity in itself, a good way to get a group to start thinking *as* a team.

Choose the requirements. First present your class with two or three requirements that the group needs to meet, in order to have room for a particular *ImaginACTION* activity or set of activities. For example, here are four suggested requirements for many of the "Easy Beginnings" activities (pages 21-38):

1. All students must be able to stand in a circle without bumping into anything, including each other.

2. All students must be able to get easily to a place where they can write.

3. There must be room for students to get into groups of five.

4. The room arrangement must be one that can be achieved in less than five minutes, and in a calm, quiet, orderly manner.

Create an action plan. When the requirements are clear, divide the class into three groups, and ask each group to create a room design that will meet the listed requirements. (Where will students put the desks? Where will backpacks and books go, so they can be retrieved quickly at the end of class? Where should students sit?) Then ask the groups to create an action plan for achieving that arrangement. (How can the class rearrange the room quickly and quietly? Who should do what? Is there a particular order the group should follow?)

Ask students to observe *how* their group works:

*Your task is to plan and to watch **how** you plan. What is your group doing well? What is your role in the group? What are you doing to help the group move toward the goal?*

Allow ten to fifteen minutes for groups to plan. At the end of that time, each group should have a room design and an action plan for moving the room into that design. Allow a few more minutes for each group to decide how to persuasively present its design to the class. (A single representative? A team? Who will do what?)

What happens next will depend on the group. You might vote on the three choices. You might send the groups back to the drawing board. You might combine parts from each group's plan into a fourth option.

Put the plan into action. After the design/action plan has been selected, put the plan into action. When the students have successfully rearranged the room, have them acknowledge their success with a round of applause.

Finally, ask students to write a two paragraph "reflection" paper that answers four questions:

1. What are the strengths of our group?

2. What is the area where our group needs improvement?

3. What is my contribution to the success of my group?

4. What can I do to be a better team member?

I recently received some valuable feedback from a student after I used "Creating the Right Space" with an adult class on interpersonal communications.

"I'm not used to working in a team," the student said, "but I did fine this time because we were doing something concrete. Imagining how to design a room for maximum efficiency is something I'm good at, so I felt comfortable contributing to the discussion and working with my team."

For students who are concrete or analytical thinkers, this activity sends the signal, "Imagin-ACTION has something for everyone."

b.k.

Easy Beginnings

If you are new to active learning, the activities in "Easy Beginnings" provide an excellent place to start. All of the activities are fairly low-risk, enjoyable and easy to try. It is important to remember that a vital part of active learning is the *process* itself.

Eagle Eye Switch

"Eagle Eye Switch" is a wonderful introduction to active learning because what you ask of the students is so simple. Developed by Oregon storyteller Debra Gordon-Zaslow, this silent activity helps students become more comfortable making eye contact.

Eye contact. Have the group get into a circle, according to your action plan. (See page 18.) Talk to the students about the importance of making eye contact:

What I am going to do is look around the circle, looking each person in the eye. Then I'm going to look at one person in particular. When I do, that person and I will change places. She'll move to where I am standing, and I'll move to her place in the circle.

Demonstrate the action. Then continue:

Now the person I changed places with will repeat what I just did. She will look at each person in the circle, and then at one person in particular. She will then change places with that person.

Have the person you selected complete the demonstration. Then give one last reminder before you start the activity:

Remember, every person gets a turn, so always choose someone who hasn't yet done the eagle eye switch.

"Eagle Eye Switch" is challenging because we aren't accustomed to looking at people in such a direct way, without speaking. At the end of the activity, let students talk about how hard it was to make eye contact. Then add:

The eyes really are marvelous communication tools that tell us a great deal about each other. For example, we've all seen the news reports where they're trying to obscure someone's identity by

Some middle school students I once worked with were definitely not looking forward to drama in their classroom. When I explained the objective of "Eagle Eye Switch," one boy asked, "What else do I have to do?"

I explained again that he simply had to look at each member of the group and, without speaking, signal one person in particular. He smiled for the first time since the class had started.

*"Okay. I can do **that**!" he said.*

His words set a very good tone for future activities.

b.k.

masking the person's eyes. Even with all the other identifying characteristics intact, identification is impossible without the eyes.

Though the emphasis on making eye contact varies from culture to culture, "the eyes have it" when it comes to sending a great deal of nonverbal information.

When we're uncomfortable, we find it hard to make eye contact. But when we learn to be more comfortable with eye contact, we become more effective communicators.

A successful round of "Eagle Eye Switch" is very unifying. It helps students focus and learn to work as a part of a larger group.

My Name Is a Verb

"My Name Is a Verb" is a great get-acquainted game, but it also works well when students know each other. They like it because they are dealing with something fundamental about themselves — their names. That familiarity helps make them more comfortable as they experiment with some simple pantomime in a group setting.

The basics. Have students form a circle according to your action plan. (See page 18.) Then show them the Verb Bank (Appendix, pages 107-108). The Verb Bank can be enlarged and put on the wall, made into a transparency or photocopied so that each student has a copy.

Ask each student to select a verb that starts with the same letter as his or her first name. Then explain:

*Each of you will step to the inside of the circle, one at a time, and say your name. Then you will pantomime the activity suggested by the verb you have chosen. For example, if your name is "**Sh**erry," you might pantomime "**sh**ivering." The class will try to guess your verb.*

It works very well to follow up this activity with another name game, "Three Names" (pages 26-27).

Once a term, I teach a workshop called *Briskworks*, which is a six-day immersion into drama games and performance. The participants are always intergenerational, with ages ranging from 11 years to 60-plus, and members have various levels of acting experience.

One year Bill, a 61-year-old beginner, turned to Karen, a 12-year-old acting veteran, as we were starting "My Name Is a Verb." He said, "This isn't easy for me, you know."

Karen smiled and suggested, "Pick an easy one to start. Pretend to walk on a tightrope. They'll guess 'balance' right away."

Bill followed her suggestion, which proved sound. He thanked Karen and shook her hand.

Support and respect are often a happy side effect when students take risks.

b.k.

Three Names

To feel comfortable with active learning, students need to begin with the familiar. That's why "Three Names" works so well. Students get to talk about something they know, while looking at it in a new way.

Very interesting information springs from "Three Names," even when students have known each other for years.

The basics. Have students get into a circle according to your action plan. (See page 18.) Then divide them into teams of two partners each. Talk to students about names:

If you think about who you are, your name will be somewhere in your description. Names are pretty basic to who we are.

Your partner has a name which he likes to be called. That is your most important purpose in the next few minutes: to find out what your partner most likes to be called.

Give students an example, preferably from your own life:

My first name is Barbara. My brother is six years older than me, and one year he brought home his high school yearbook with a big picture of that year's homecoming queen, Barbara Burns, whose nickname was . . . that's right . . . Bobbi. She was so beautiful. I figured it couldn't hurt, so I changed my name right then and there.

That's the kind of information we're looking for.

Ask students also to find out what other names their partner has been called — *friendly* nicknames only. If their partner doesn't have a nickname, ask students to find out something else about the person's name:

Maybe your partner was named after someone from a story or after someone's favorite aunt. Maybe she always wished for a different name, or maybe there is a funny story about how the parents picked the name. See what you can find out.

Explain that students will move outside the circle to interview each other. When they come back to the circle, each set of partners will introduce each other. Emphasize what they will be sharing:

1. *Tell your partner's name and three names that he or she likes to be called.*

2. *If the person doesn't have three names, tell us something interesting about the person's name.*

3. *Either way, finish by telling us what your partner most likes to be called.*

Even students who are self-conscious can easily do this activity. A simple response like this is fine:

This is John. He doesn't really have any nicknames, and he was named after President John F. Kennedy. He likes to be called John.

You might try . . . Extend this activity further by asking students to pick one of their own nicknames, or a particular way of pronouncing one of their names (Hen-RY or HEN-ry, for example). Ask:

When would you be most likely to hear this name or this pronunciation? Who would say it? Tell us the circumstances, and then demonstrate what would be said.

Many students will demonstrate how their parents say their names when they are in trouble, as in:

Michael Anthony Cunningham, did you drink the last soda?

Other situations could be a coach yelling at a basketball player:

CUNningham! Get in there!

or a sister begging her big brother for a favor:

Mikie, please? Please drive me to the mall?

I have used "Three Names" quite often in groups where everybody supposedly knows everybody. At one faculty in-service at a small private school in Northern California, a history teacher who had seemed distant and remote revealed that his nickname as a child had been "Sparky."

Later that day at lunch, I heard a young math teacher call out, "Sparky, can I sit at your table?" The math teacher had taught at the school for three years and had always wanted to approach the respected older teacher. After "Three Names," he finally felt comfortable enough to do it.

b.k.

Mirrors

Poets call the eyes the windows to the soul. It's no wonder, then, that eye contact is sometimes difficult for people. "Mirrors" points out that difficulty and helps students manage it. It is also an excellent exercise in focusing attention entirely on the matter at hand.

Mirroring motion. Have the class get into a circle according to your action plan. (See page 18.) Divide the group into teams of two and have partners face each other, standing about 18 inches apart. Ask them to hold their elbows close to their sides and raise their forearms and hands so that their palms are facing their partners' palms. Explain:

Touch your palms to your partner's palms —that's it. Keep them together . . . Now pull the hands back so that they do not touch, but are about two inches apart . . . There. You have just "mirrored" each other.

Explain that one person in each team will start by being the initiator. That person will choose actions for his or her partner to mirror. When you call "Change," the other person will become the initiator, without breaking the motion of the activities. Explain further:

Partners should look into each other's eyes. The initiator begins moving and, still focusing on the initiator's eyes, the follower follows the movement.

There are three ground rules to mirroring your partner:

1. *Partners must be silent.*

2. *They never touch.*

3. *They never fall down.*

In moving, partners can use facial expressions and change levels by bending or stretching. Movements need to be slow enough so that they are easy to follow. As the activity is in progress, you may want to do some side coaching (See page 16):

There is a temptation to laugh. That's okay. Don't worry about it. Just take a breath and you'll find it easier to keep your focus. . .

Change.

Any basketball fans in here? Did you ever see a player running down the court facing the basket and, without turning around, just reach out to catch a basketball thrown by someone running behind? How does the player know that the ball is being thrown?

This activity is sort of like that. Part of what is happening is that you are training yourself to use your peripheral vision, your side to side vision. You are also learning to relax and focus so that you can be ready for whatever happens.

Change.

Now, without stopping, I want you to slow your movements to about half as fast as you are moving now. Sloooowwww dowwwwwn. Good.

Change. And keep that very easy movement. Good.

Change. And now, go even more slowly, half as fast as you are moving now.

Change. Good. I see some really good focus here. I see some of you stretching and experimenting with levels of movement. That's great. Keep it simple enough for your partner to follow.

Change. (Pause for 10 seconds.)

Change. (Pause again.)

Change (Pause once more.) *And stop. Good.*

Discussion. Ask students to raise their hands if they found this activity difficult to do. Many students probably did. Ask why. Some will talk about the difficulty of keeping eye contact.

If you find eye contact difficult, that is very natural. If you don't find it difficult, you have a useful skill. Is there anything you can say that will help others find a way to make eye contact easier?

I once tried "Mirrors" at a treatment center for adolescent boys. At first their resistance was incredible. The boys giggled. They argued. They said, "This is so stupid."

I continued with the exercise. I kept insisting that they stay with it, saying, "Give yourselves the opportunity to reap the benefits from this. Take a breath. That will help with the giggles."

At last, nearly every team of two found its focus, and the boys were very proud of themselves. They had overcome their embarrassment and stayed with the exercise, despite its difficulty.

b.k.

Sometimes students will point out that you can look away slightly and focus on the forehead for a moment and then return to the eyes. Others will point out that the "chemistry" of each team has a lot to do with how comfortable the team members are. Point out that life is like that too:

Life often throws us into situations where we must work with a partner we may or may not be comfortable with. Making eye contact is good practice for people beginning to work together.

After discussion, you can repeat the activity with new partners, or have students keep the same partners.

You might try . . . It's easy to give "Mirrors" variety. You might try the following instructions:

This time when you move, move like a robot, very mechanically. Make every movement separate and distinct.

or:

This time move as if something is holding you back and there is tremendous resistance to every move you make.

Something Good

It's easy to get caught up in looking at the negative and ignoring all the good that is happening around us. "Something Good" helps students shift into a positive mode of thinking.

The basics. Start by asking each person to tell something good that has already happened today:

It has to be about something that you're involved in or something that made you feel good.

A statement can be made only one time. If somebody says what you were going to say, think of something else or change the statement just a little.

After everyone has shared, talk about how easy it is to say something negative. We like to complain, and many of us often fall into a "poor me" attitude. Most people have an easier time coming up with something *bad* that has happened than something good. The important thing is that students understand that "What we are able to see is what we get." If we are able to see the positive, our experiences actually become more positive because our perception has changed.

Remind students that "something good" doesn't have to be about winning the lottery or being the fastest or the best. A very small moment can still be positive and important.

I love to do "Something Good" first thing in the morning. Students have had less time for something good to happen, and it's more of a stretch to think of something positive.

Once I had a teenager come to class late, looking very grumpy. She announced that there was nothing good that had happened to her so far that morning.

"Don't ignore the obvious," I told her.

She rolled her eyes a little and said, "Okay, so I woke up."

Another student immediately responded, "That qualifies as a good thing!"

b.k.

Restate

A good guideline for anyone to follow is this one: Say what you want, not what you don't want.

Students need practice in creating positive pictures in their minds. "Restate" helps them learn to turn negative statements into positive ones.

The basics. Tell the students about one of the viewpoints of the great director Alfred Hitchcock:

Hitchcock used to say that the best way to get someone to fall down a flight of stairs is to say, "Don't fall, don't fall." Why? Because you are creating a picture of falling.

If we really don't want someone to fall down the stairs, a more effective statement is, "Take it easy," or, "Take the steps one at a time." Then you create a picture of a person taking the time to be careful.

Discuss Hitchcock's statement with the class. Then ask students to change the following negative statements so that they create positive pictures instead of negative ones:

- Negative statement:
  I know I won't like it.
  Positive restatements:
  I'll give it a chance.
  It may turn out better than I think it will.

- Negative statement:
  Nobody likes me.
  Positive restatements:
  I like myself.
  I have one good friend.

Divide the class into teams of three. Give each team an index card with a sentence that needs to be restated to create a positive image. Ask students to restate the sentences so that they say what is *wanted* instead of what is *not* wanted. (Repeat the same sentence on more than one card. That way groups will see how other groups restated the same words.)

Here are some negative statements you can use for the cards:

- I'm sure I'll be embarrassed.

- I'm so clumsy.

- I always get a cold this time every year.

- This isn't my day.

- I can't say "no" to my friends.

- What a loser I am.

- I'm sure she will say "no."

- I know I'll have a terrible time if I go.

- I'll never pass that test.

- I'm not good enough to get on the team.

- I can't get along with my parents.

- I can never win that election.

- Nothing good ever happens to me.

- No one listens to me.

- There's no way I can do that!

Whenever I try "Restate" with a group, I stress that students should "Say what you want and not what you don't want."

One day I had a student arrive with a few examples of "Say what you don't want" statements he had heard made to children when he went to the park:

- *You'll fall off and break you're head.*

- *If you go on the big slide, the kids will be mean to you.*

- *Don't climb too high.*

- *Don't push.*

*"Little kids really get it in a big way," he said. "I probably heard the words **can't** and **don't** a hundred times apiece!"*

b.k.

Trapped

"Trapped" is an exercise that can be done again and again, with the same group. The results will be different each time.

Creating a scene. Divide the class into teams of two people each. Then say:

*The word of the day is **trapped**. With your partner, build a thirty-second to one-minute-long scene that shows the essence of the word **trapped**. In your presentation, the most important thing is clarity. Your scene should have a beginning, a middle and an end. It should communicate the essence of **trapped** very clearly.*

Of course students will have questions. Here are some of the most frequent ones:

- *Can we use words? (Yes.)*

- *Do we have to use words? (No.)*

- *Do we have to get **un**trapped? (No.)*

- *How long does it have to be again? (No longer than one minute.)*

Point out that traps don't have to be physical, like being **trapped** in an elevator. A person can also be **trapped** in a lie, for example. Remind students to look for examples that are beyond the obvious.

Allow students a few minutes to prepare. Then have each team present its scene for the class.

You might try . . . Although it is effective to use the word "trapped" several times with the same group, you can also try different words and phrases as the essence of the scene. Here are a few that work well:

- A bad habit

- The letter

- Time out

- Forgive
- A misunderstanding
- Personal best
- Dissolve
- Great idea

Another idea is to take your weekly vocabulary list, if you use one, and put each word on a card. Ask each team of two to draw a card and then develop a short scene depicting the essence of that vocabulary word. In this case, students should *not* say the word in the course of the scene. Guessing is part of the fun (and learning).

I have been amazed at the levels some students achieve with "Trapped." My favorite memory involves a team of two students named Emily and Suzanne.

Emily played the role of an injured young woman telling her best friend why she had a black eye. Although her boyfriend had hit her, she told her friend that the black eye resulted from a fall on her bike. The girl felt trapped in an abusive relationship.

It turned out that in real life Emily really did have a boyfriend who verbally and physically abused her. After class she asked me about crisis intervention programs.

Emily's creative exploration led to real life discoveries.

b.k.

Two People Who Never Should Have Met

"Two People Who Never Should Have Met" is an excellent introduction to the whole subject of conflict. It's all about people having differences and viewing the same situation in completely different ways.

Talking about opposites. Talk with your students about the word "incompatibility." What does it mean?

Someone may point out that "incompatibility" is often given as a reason for divorce. Or sometimes college roommates have to find new roommates because they are "incompatible." Ask:

What might make two people incompatible?

Someone who is a night owl may find it difficult to be married to a morning person. Someone who is tidy may find it very frustrating to live with a person who is always leaving a mess. Quite often, of course, incompatibility results from opposite personality or character traits.

Creating a scene. Divide the class into teams of two students each. Then ask each team to develop a 30-60 second scene based on a meeting between incompatible opposites. Students may either talk or be silent in the scene.

Give the class an example:

Someone who is easy-going could get into a fender-bender with an uptight, always-in-a-hurry person. How would each of the two people see the situation? How would each of them react?

Have some ideas in reserve for helping any teams that have difficulty. A few ideas:

- Messy vs. neat

- Reader vs. video game player

- Classical music lover vs. rock music lover

- Cheerful vs. sullen

- Calm vs. uptight

- Talkative vs. quiet

- Affectionate vs. distant

- Punctual vs. late

- City dweller vs. country dweller

- Fashion conscious vs. "grab whatever is clean"

Allow students some time to prepare. Then have each group present its scene to the class.

Just in case. Remind students that it is all right if someone uses an idea that they were going to use. They should go ahead and present their idea anyway, bringing their own flare to the scene.

Here's an example of a "Two People Who Never Should Have Met" scene created by two eighth grade boys. They wanted to show two college roommates who couldn't communicate. One was always making a point, but the other could never understand it.

Scott: *I have something I need to talk over with you, Ryan.*

Ryan: *What's up?*

Scott: *I need to study, but you're always making noise.*

Ryan: *So, what are you saying, Scott?*

Scott: *I'm saying that you play your music too loud, you talk too much, and you bring your friends over at all hours.*

Ryan: *So, what are you trying to tell me?*

Scott: *(Becoming exasperated) I can't sleep, I can't study, I can't think. You are driving me crazy!*

Ryan: *Because if you ever have a problem, you can always talk to me.*

Scott: *(sighing) Right. Thanks, Ryan. That's good to know.*

Ryan: *Give me five, dude.*

Scott: *(resigned) Right on.*

b.k.

Slow Walk

People usually walk very quickly. We all move from place to place without particularly noticing how we move — unless something like a sprained ankle forces us to notice. With "Slow Walk," slow motion gives students a whole new awareness of how they move.

The activity is a good one to use when emotions run high, as they often do when creativity is unleashed. It helps students calm down and focus very clearly, in a concrete way, on something familiar.

Moving in slow motion. Have students arrange the room so that there is a lot of space for movement, according to your action plan. (See page 18.) Explain that they are going to be experimenting with slow motion. Stress that the two rules for this activity are "Don't talk," and "Move slowly."

Have students stand in various places around the room. Then give them these instructions:

When I tell you to begin, start walking. Make sure to pay attention to those around you so that you don't bump into one another. And remember, move slowly — and without talking.

Let students walk for about two minutes. With 30 seconds left, ask them to slow down to half speed.

For discussion. Ask students what they noticed during the exercise. You will likely hear responses like these:

- *Moving slowly affected my balance.*

- *I noticed that my arms usually move.*

- *I thought it was relaxing.*

"Slow Walk" helps students see the value of looking at ordinary things in a new way. It is a good activity to repeat, increasing the time with each repetition.

Body Language

"Body Language" includes many activities that help students learn to communicate more effectively. They gain an understanding of how body language, tone of voice and facial expressions can be even more important than words in communicating a clear message.

Communicating through Body Language

It's important to know that we cannot *not* communicate. Even when we aren't speaking, our facial expressions and body positions send a message. "Body Language" helps students understand that words are only one of the tools we use to communicate our feelings, thoughts and attitudes.

A look at body language. To begin this activity, say:

Think about how people communicate without using words. For example, how could you say **STOP** *without using words?*

Have several students demonstrate non-verbal ways to communicate *STOP!* For example, a person could hold both hands straight out at arms length, palms vertical and facing out.

After the demonstrations, ask:

What does it look like to say **STOP** *and really mean it? Suppose you're telling your brother to leave you alone, and you want your* **STOP** *to say "I mean it!" How would that look?*

Have volunteers demonstrate their ideas. Then go on:

What does it look like to say **STOP** *and not really mean it? Suppose you're kidding around with a friend, and you want your* **STOP** *to say, "I'm not serious." How would that look?*

Again, have volunteers demonstrate.

> *Body language is not universal in meaning. For example, the "okay" gesture with the thumb and forefinger joined to form a circle is a signal of appreciation in the United States. In France and Belgium, however, it says, "You're a zero." In Greece and Turkey the same gesture is a lewd sexual invitation.*
>
> *In Italy, the signal for "go away" is exactly the same as the sign most North Americans use when saying "Come here." Pointing can be unclear in Puerto Rico, where it is common to pucker lips to point directions, instead of using fingers.*
>
> *I once got "caught" when my ignorance of the Hmong culture produced an embarrassing situation. At a performance, I was invited to the front of the room. There were children sitting on the floor, so I stepped over them, exposing the bottom of my foot to them. A gasp shot through the audience. It turns out that holding the bottom of my foot visible over the top of their heads was extremely offensive in their culture.*
>
> *b.k.*

Talk with students about what helped the volunteers communicate their messages. Students should understand that facial expressions, body positions and movement all contribute to making a message clear.

Using body language. Have students experiment with using only body language (no words) to communicate. Give each student one of the following messages to try to communicate to the class:

- What a good smell.
- What a bad smell.
- I love that music.
- I hate that music.
- The stove is hot.
- I'm angry.
- I like you.
- Lassie, go home.
- What a dumb idea.
- What a great idea.
- Give me a break.
- Get off my back.
- Hurry up.
- Take it easy.
- I can't hear you.
- I think I did a great job.
- Please be quiet.
- That was a great performance.
- I don't feel good.
- I'm hungry.
- I'm thirsty.
- I'm scared.
- I'm depressed.
- I have a secret to tell you.
- It's time to go.
- I'm lost.
- I want to be alone.
- Stay down, or they'll see you.
- I don't get it.
- Follow me.

You might try . . . Talk with students about how body language can affect the outcome of a situation. For example, if the principal is talking to a student about his misbehavior, the student could say, "I'm sorry, ma'am." If he stands tall and makes eye contact, his words might come across as sincere. If he slouches and looks away or shakes his head from side to side, his words might seem disrespectful.

The results? If the principal believes that the student's apology is sincere, it may raise her level of trust in the student.

With the class, brainstorm a list of situations where body language could have a big effect on the meaning or outcome. Just a few examples:

- A parent tells a child to do the dishes.
- A teenager agrees to go with the family to visit weird Aunt Harriet.
- A teenager tells his parents that he wants to be left alone.
- A person congratulates a good friend on an opposing team for winning.

Then explain:

We are going to do quick demonstrations of each situation we came up with, using different body language each time.

Body language, facial expressions and tone of voice all contribute to non-verbal communication. This time we're going to concentrate on body language and facial expression, so it is important to keep your tone of voice the same in each demonstration. Don't change your pitch or tone; just try to keep your voice neutral. That way we can concentrate on how body language and facial expressions affect the message in each scene.

Point out that students in each demonstration should react to the body language and facial expressions they see. For example, if a teenager puts his arm around a parent and says, "I need to be left alone for a little while," the parent might respond with a hug. If the teenager waves a fist in the parent's face while saying, "I need to be left alone for a little while," he might get an angry response.

For discussion. Discuss the different outcomes of various kinds of body language. Do students see any patterns emerging in the demonstrations?

Observation

Observation is key to communication. It's amazing how many people don't notice basic things about others around them. Ask someone, "How do you think Pete felt about that?" and you might hear, "I don't have a clue" — even though Pete was showing every sign of being embarrassed. When people really observe one another, they communicate better.

With "Observation," each student observes a person and records details, especially details about the person's movement and body language. Then class members try to duplicate some of the actions they observed.

Watching and writing. Ask students to complete the following writing assignment:

Outside of class, choose an individual and watch that person very closely for a period of time, probably about half an hour. Choose someone who is busy at an activity that will take awhile —perhaps a restaurant worker, a mother shopping with children, a speaker addressing a group, your father grilling hamburgers, a teenager waiting in a long line, for example. Your job, during that time, is to record details about the person. Answer the following:

1. *Describe what the person looks like. (Male? Female? Tall? Short? Blonde? Brunette? etc.) Be specific.*

2. *Describe the way the person moves. (Does he have an interesting walk, way of sitting, way of standing? Does she have a slow or fast pace? Is the person picking up, putting down or carrying anything?)*

3. *Describe the person's non-verbal communication. (Facial expressions, distinctive gestures, etc.)*

After students hand in their written observations, go through them, looking for descriptions of *action*. (The assignment asks students to describe appearance as well, but that's just to help them focus on details. What is really important in this activity are the details about the person's actions.)

Select portions of each student's work that show action and reproduce them. You might highlight the selections with a colored marker, photocopy them or retype them.

For example, on one paper you might select this description:

The person had a nervous habit of running fingers through hair. Used right hand.

On another, you might mark this one:

Crossed her legs and jiggled her right leg nervously. Shoe slipped loose, but she let it hang, swinging back and forth, from her big toe.

Hand the selections out, randomly, to class members. Explain that each student, in turn, is to come forward and demonstrate the action described in the selection he or she received.

You might try . . . As the class reads stories and novels, you might try having students collect "do-able" traits from the characters they are reading about. If you read about a character who bites her lower lip, for example, that action might be included on the do-able trait list. After you have a substantial list of traits, have students demonstrate them. It's fun to try to match the traits demonstrated with the characters the class has been reading about.

Once, when I was using "Observation" with a high school drama class, a young woman gave a very clear demonstration of someone trying to give instructions. She used no words, but her movements were so distinctive that everyone guessed correctly who had been the subject of the observation.

It was me. For a long time after that, I was very conscious of my gestures and movement whenever I gave instructions.

b.k.

Tableau

A perfect time to try out "Tableau" is after someone has been chided for a negative attitude and cries out, "But I didn't say anything!" The activity shows how communication can occur without any words at all.

Tableau is also fun to use when a group seems to have some excess energy to expend. It provides lots of opportunity for action, thinking and discussion.

Creating a tableau. Divide the class into several smaller groups. Then write the word *tableau* on the chalkboard. Say:

Think of a tableau as a still picture made with people. For example, imagine a famous painting like American Gothic — the one of the farm couple, with the man holding a pitchfork and the woman looking stern. If you recreated it with living people, you would have a tableau.

Today we're going to create several tableaux, or still pictures. Our tableaux are going to communicate very specific messages.

Demonstrate the building of a tableau by using a group of four or five volunteers:

We're going to do a tableau called "A Day at the Zoo." We'll ask Michael to be a gorilla. Megan, Rosa and Scott will be people outside the cage looking in. Each of them will have a different expression. Megan will be pointing and laughing. Scott, you will be trying to imitate the gorilla. Rosa, you will react by looking closely at the gorilla. Ready?

Now, everyone perform your roles. When I call "freeze," stop and hold your position. Then we will have a tableau.

After the demonstration, have each group create a tableau. Say:

Now, I'll come around and give a tableau subject to each group. Your job will be to create a tableau illustrating the subject and communicating its meaning clearly. Remember, everyone in your group must have a role in your tableau.

Write the names of tableau subjects on index cards ahead of time, or whisper the subjects to each group. Here are some tableau subjects that work well:

- Pick up this mess.

- Don't mess with me.

- We're cool.

- The big game.

- It's okay.

- After exercise class.

- We're really sorry.

- Someone's singing off-key.

- The new kid.

- Taking a test.

- Losers.

- Winners.

It's a good idea to have "Losers" and "Winners" as the last two tableaux presented. You can point out the different body language in these two messages very clearly. Also, they make a perfect transition into the next activity, "Snapshots" (page 48).

You might try . . . Instead of giving students a lot of time to prepare, try giving them just five seconds to get into the tableau. Say:

Five, four, three, two, one . . . FREEZE

Another idea is to use other students in the class as "sculptors" instead of having participants form their own tableaux. Ask for volunteers to come to the front and stand in a line, facing the class. Say:

The name of this tableau is "We're cool." I need sculptors to come forward and move these group members into that statement. Move a leg or an arm, or help them change their facial expressions to say "we're cool."

> *It's amazing, but in every country I've traveled in, in every age group, there is a certain posture — a little slouched, with one leg slightly forward, head cocked to the side — that means "cool."*
>
> *b.k.*

Snapshot

Everyone loves a winner. With "Snapshot" students create living snapshots of winning moments, starring themselves. The activity coordinates writing and action to help students focus on the positive.

Feeling like a winner. Ask students to recall times when they felt like winners. With the entire group, brainstorm a list of situations where someone could feel like a winner — like sports events, artistic performances, family gatherings, good times with friends, etc. (See also, "Something Good," page 31).

Ask students to write for five minutes about a time they felt like a winner. What happened? Who was there? How did they feel?

Then have them write about a winning moment they would *like* to take place. What would they like to happen? Who would be there? How do they think they would feel?

Divide the class into small groups and explain:

Now it's time for some action. Today we are going to create snapshots, but not the kind of snapshots you take with a camera. These are going to be living snapshots of winning moments.

Each of you will become the "director" of a snapshot that shows a winning moment starring **you** *— only you won't be in your own snapshot. You will choose someone in the group to play the part of you.*

Explain that the snapshots will be "freeze frames" that show a moment in time. Demonstrate:

Sam, let's imagine that you're playing the part of me. I'm running in a track meet and I am exhausted, but I am winning. Lori, you're going to be coming in second. Steve, you're the guy with the stopwatch who watches the finish line. Melissa, you'll play the part of my sister, who came to the track meet to cheer me on.

Arrange the students so that they demonstrate the action; then say "freeze."

Explain that students can direct snapshots of winning moments that actually happened to them, or of winning moments they *wish* would happen to them. Then give the groups time to prepare a snapshot for each person's winning moment, directed by that person.

As each group presents its snapshots to the class, the director explains what the audience is seeing.

After discussion, have students go back to their original writing. Have them add more details and refine their work, to turn in.

You might try . . . The ideal is for all students to have the experience of creating a snapshot and explaining it to the class. However, another possibility is to have students choose one or two events in each group to become snapshots.

After students have directed snapshots of winning moments, you might try having them make snapshots of other moments, like "a moment of happiness" or "a moment of laughter" or "a moment of embarrassment."

I used to do "Snapshots" without the writing assignment. I would show students the track meet example, and then every snapshot created in the entire class would have something to do with a track meet or a sporting event.

Adding the writing assignment helped a lot. Students have time to think and to put down details of their own experiences. The resulting snapshots are much more interesting and varied.

b.k.

Body Language

Emotional Orchestra

Non-verbal communication can include both facial expressions and sounds. People often use the two together to help communicate a message. For example, laughter and a smile can communicate happiness.

With "Emotional Orchestra," students follow a conductor's instructions as they produce sounds associated with different emotions. The activity is perfect for large groups, and it is definitely a lot of fun.

Getting ready. Ask students, silently, to choose one of the following very general emotions:

- happy

- sad

- angry

- excited

Call out each emotion and ask students to raise their hands if that's the one they picked. Get all the "happy" people together, all the "sad" people together, etc. Then say:

Many emotions have sounds associated with them. For example, if you were feeling annoyed with someone, you might make the sound of a heavy sigh as you rolled your eyes.

Think of a sound that "says" your emotion. Everyone in the "happy" group, think of a sound that says "happy" to you. If you're in the "sad" group, think of a sound that says "sad" to you. If you're in the "angry" group, think of an angry sound, and if you're in the "excited" group, think of an excited sound. Your sound doesn't have to be the same sound others in your group are making.

Everybody ready? Okay, all together now — make your sound.

Explain that you are going to demonstrate some conducting signals. Raise your arms to signal getting louder (crescendo). Put your palms down and lower your arms to indicate getting quieter (decrescendo).

Move your arms rapidly to indicate getting faster, and move your hands apart in a "s-t-r-r-e-t-t-c-h-h" signal to indicate getting slower. Finally, hold both palms outward in a "halt" sign to mean stop altogether.

Creating the orchestra. Explain that you are going to be the orchestra conductor, and the students are going to be the orchestra members. The sounds they create will be the "sad," "happy," "angry" or "excited" sounds of their groups.

Start by asking each group, one at a time, to make its sounds together. Have each group follow your conducting signals to get louder, quieter, faster, slower, etc.

Then start conducting all the groups simultaneously. Have one group get louder and louder while another becomes quieter and quieter. Stop one group altogether while bringing up the volume on another. Have two groups speed up and two groups slow down. See how well the students can follow your conducting instructions.

You might try . . . If anyone in the class is interested in conducting, let her give it a try.

You might also try using the sounds from instruments in an actual orchestra first, before you do the emotional orchestra. Ask students to choose an instrument from your imaginary collection of instruments. Then group all percussion instruments together, all woodwinds, all strings, all brass, etc. Have each student choose a sound representative of his instrument group.

Demonstrate the conducting signals. Then proceed as described above, giving the different instrument groups varying instructions to follow. After the group is comfortable with the musical orchestra, go ahead and set up the emotional orchestra.

Once, when I visited an eighth grade health class and tried "Emotional Orchestra," an apathetic girl in an ultra-popular clique really resisted. I carried on.

"It's okay," I said. "Just stand up there with your group. No problem. It's pretty silly, so just do the best you can."

She had picked "happy" as her emotion. At first she stood with the other "happy" students and shifted her weight from one foot to the other, rolling her eyes. But the other students were participating, some even exuberantly, and obviously having a good time. No one was looking at her because everyone was busy being in the orchestra.

For some reason, the girl decided to join in. Her expression of happiness was "YEA!" She was tentative at first, and then she actually clapped her hands and said "YEA!" with enthusiasm.

I know that if I had looked at that young girl and smiled as she said "YEA!" she might have stopped cold. The spark of creativity is a fragile one. A gust of wind might blow it out, or it might set it ablaze. I feel very humble in its presence.

I did feel very pleased later when I heard the health teacher telling a colleague, "Courtney halfway enjoyed herself in class today. It was wonderful!"

b.k.

Three Ways to Say It

Tone of voice is a very important part of communication. People often pay attention to the words they say but give no thought to *how* they are saying them. They don't understand that tone and emphasis help give words meaning. "Three Ways to Say It" helps show students the importance tone of voice can play in communication.

Getting ready. It's easy to think of words as units with fixed meanings. In reality, however, words are not so easy to pin down. Ask:

When we put a bunch of words together, what gives them meaning?

Students will probably have many answers, like "How we say them" or "Everybody speaking the same language."

Write the words "That's great" on the board. Ask:

Look at these words. Could we say them in more than one way?

Students will probably be quick to demonstrate different ways of saying the words. If they aren't, demonstrate by saying "that's great" with enthusiasm and then with sarcasm. Add:

"That's great" (said with enthusiasm) and "That's great" (said with sarcasm) mean two very different things. The words could also sound hesitant or amazed or . . . Well, the list could go on and on.

Follow up with another group of words, like "That sounds like fun." Again, ask:

Could we say these words more than one way?

Again, allow students to demonstrate.

Acting out. Ask for three volunteers to come in front of the class. Give them all the same sentence or phrase from the phrase list below. (Write the phrases on index cards or just whisper them to the students.) Explain that each student is to say the phrase in a different way, so that the meaning changes. Give them a moment; then have the students demonstrate.

When the class understands the directions, have students get into teams of three. Give each team an item from the suggestion list below, and have each team member interpret the same item so that it has a different meaning.

The suggestion list:

- Oh, really ?

- Give me a break.

- I'd love to hear about it.

- You did what?

- I'm sure you think so.

- Don't worry about it.

- That's what you think.

- It's nice to hear your voice.

- I never expected to see you here.

- May I help you?

- Oh, I'm fine.

- Let's forget about it, okay?

- Everybody's having such a good time.

- Is that what you're wearing to the dance?

- That's just like you to do something like that.

You might also try . . . "Three Ways to Say It" can also be an individual activity, with each person demonstrating three ways to say the same statement.

You might also try having students present each statement in context. Students give their statements as part of a situation they have created and are acting out.

In an informal mediation between two arguing friends, I used a form of "Three Ways to Say It." First I asked each for an explanation of what had happened.

Jan said, "He asked if I liked his idea, and I said, 'It's okay,' but he got mad."

Craig said, "Then I said, 'That's great,' and she started yelling at me."

Before we went on to discuss the idea and how Jan really felt about it, I asked Jan to say "It's okay," and Craig to respond with "That's great." After they did it once, I asked them to do it again, giving the words an entirely different meaning, and then again a third time.

The third time, Jan rolled her eyes, looked away, and said in an irritated tone, "It's okay."

"That's exactly what you did before," Craig responded. "You rolled your eyes and looked away."

Their awareness finally moved them beyond what their words had said. They both acknowledged that their actual communication had been in tone and expression, not words.

b.k.

Body Language

Gibberish Argument

"Gibberish Argument" grew from an exercise called "How to Start an Argument" in *Playfair,* a popular book of noncompetitive games by Matt Weinstein and Joel Goodwin (Impact Publishers, 1980).

Even the most reserved students will often respond to this activity. However, pay special attention to how you group students. Putting two quiet students together can make it difficult.

Nonsensical talk. To introduce the word "gibberish," read aloud the poem "Jabberwocky," by Lewis Carroll. Ask:

What is this poem about? How do you know? What makes this a poem? What kind of language is this?

Gibberish is, of course, nonsensical talk. The talk may sound word-like, but the words have no meaning.

Ask for two volunteers to do a gibberish improvisation. The two will stage an argument, talking entirely in gibberish. Explain:

Katie, you will begin the argument with an angry gibberish barb or insult. Owen, you will respond, in gibberish, and escalate the argument. In other words, make it more intense. Continue back and forth, making the argument peak, and then wind it down as you figure out, in gibberish, how to resolve the argument.

After the argument, ask the volunteers if they had any sense of being in a real argument. Ask the class:

We didn't know the meaning of their words, but we knew they were arguing. What told us that?

Students should point out that facial expressions, posture, tone of voice, motions and proximity to one another all helped demonstrate that the conversation was an argument.

More gibberish. For a follow-up activity, divide the class into small groups. Assign each group a "scene situation" from the list below. (See also "List of Situations," page 113.) Then have the groups enact their scenes, using only gibberish for "words." Remind students that every scene needs a beginning, a middle and an end.

The situations:

- A flight attendant prepares passengers for an emergency landing.

- Everyone in an entire restaurant thinks that the entree has too much hot sauce.

- Noticing that a customer stole an item, a store clerk tells both coworkers and the supervisor.

- At a dance, one person is interested in another, tries to find out if the feeling is mutual and then approaches the person to ask for a dance.

- A group of inept robbers holds up a bank.

- A group of young children attends the carnival and enjoys eating cotton candy, shooting ducks, trying various rides and other activities.

- Male and female models prepare for a runway fashion show, with the designer directing.

- Friends with different tastes try to decide on one video to rent for the evening.

- A photographer tries to get a family ready for a group photograph.

After each scene, talk with the class about how clearly the points came across in the presentation. Students will soon see how important tone, movements and attitudes are in conveying a point. In other words, meanings are in people, not in words.

I once directed a project called "Hands Across the Ocean" (or "Rukea Chedez Okean"), which brought together actors from Siberia and actors from Oregon. While we shared the language of the stage, most of the Oregonians spoke very little Russian, and most of the Siberians spoke very little English.

Sometimes we would have an interpreter, but often we were left to stumble through rehearsals, trying to communicate subtle concepts with hand gestures, broad movements and the few words we had learned in common. It was exhausting.

At one rehearsal we played "Gibberish." We had been trying so hard to communicate that our brows were furrowed with the effort. But one by one, as the Russian actors began to understand what I was telling them, their faces relaxed and they were eager to try the game. When we started to speak gibberish, we all began to laugh and felt energized to continue the rehearsal.

b.k.

Improvisation

We "wing it" every day. Improvisation turns winging it into an art form.

The activities in this chapter focus on working with what we're given and paying attention to details. While some of the activities are challenging, most can be adapted to any group. Some of the activities even depart from "pure improv" to give students a bit of preparation time.

Say Yes

"Say Yes" is an improvisation standard developed by Keith Johnstone, a leader in the field of improvisation and author of *Impro: Improvisation and the Theatre* (Routledge Chapman Hall, 1979). "Say Yes" is a wonderful barrier breaker for large groups, and it makes a perfect introduction to improvisation activities.

With this version of the activity, students find a way to say "Yes!" to all improvisation ideas presented to them. The activity can be a lot of fun, and it helps create a positive momentum that encourages students to take risks.

Thinking about Robin Williams. Many students have seen comedian Robin Williams improvising on television. When someone shouts out an idea, he never turns it down. He accepts each idea as a gift and goes with it, turning a morsel into a feast as he improvises. Explain to students that they are going to copy Robin Williams by refusing to say the word "no" during this exercise.

The disguised "no." Point out that there are, of course, ways of saying "no" without saying "no." There are obvious refusals like "No way!" or "Not on your life." But there are also more subtle refusals. Ask students to imagine this conversation:

Jody: *Let's take a kite and go the park.*

Sam: *Kites are bogus.*

Jody: *Not this one. It's bright blue and red.*

Sam: *I hate red.*

Jody: *Well, it's supposed to be a great day for flying a kite.*

Sam: *By the time we get there, the wind will probably die down.*

You get the picture. It is difficult to stay enthusiastic about an idea in the face of an "I have a million ways to say no" expert.

Before you introduce improvisation, talk with students about how "no" dampens enthusiasm for just about any project. Saying "yes," on the other hand, opens up new possibilities.

Now for the action. The whole classroom is the stage for "Say Yes," and everyone takes part at the same time. You may move the desks to the side of the room, or you can have students perform in the aisles between the desks. (See also "Creating the Right Space," page 18.)

Explain that you will shout out an instruction. Everyone is to say, "Yes! Let's . . ." and repeat the instruction. Then they are to begin doing whatever was suggested.

For example, you might give this instruction:

Let's walk backwards.

Students answer:

Yes!

They begin walking backwards. Then one of the students comes up with another idea:

Let's play tennis.

The class answers:

Yes!

Everyone starts going through the motions of playing tennis.

While it is important that no one says "no," it's also important that no one is asked to do anything inappropriate. It's a good idea to talk about your expectations before you start this activity. For example, you might rule out anything that would insult an individual or a group, or that would involve risqué behavior. (See also "The A word," page 17.)

You might want to have a system for who gets to shout out an instruction, just so you don't have chaos on your hands. It can be something simple, like tossing a Nerf ball to someone, who then gets to come up with the next instruction. Or you might simply call on people to take a turn.

Call a Place

"Call a Place" involves you, as side coach (See page 16), calling out the names of various places to be, like "the beach" or "a bus station" or "a fruit stand." Then you add details and questions to help students create characters to inhabit those places.

The activity provides a great way to begin looking at empathy. The question "How does it feel to walk for a few minutes in someone else's shoes?" can lead to thought-provoking discussion and growth.

Round one. Begin by having each student find a spot in the room where he will be "performing." With this activity, all students are participating at the same time.

Explain that you will call out the name of a place. Students first "go" to that place in their minds. For example, you might say:

You're at the beach.

Working in her own spot, each student then creates a character to be in that place. You will help by calling out details and questions that will help students "see" who they want to be. As you talk, they become someone else, using body language, movement, facial expressions, etc. — but no words.

You might say something like this:

It's very warm outside, and the sand is a little hot on the beach.

What are you doing? Who are you? Are you young, old, fast, slow? Do you love being out in the sun or are you uncomfortable in all this heat? Go ahead . . . Start "becoming" who you are . . .

It's a little crowded out here today, how do you feel about that? Do you like meeting new people or would you rather be left alone?

You may continue these questions for quite awhile, allowing students to layer on details and round out their characters. It is a good idea to have a number of questions ready, so that you will feel

> *Details are important in creating a realistic character. When I was a student actor, one of my favorite directors turned to me suddenly at a rehearsal and asked a question of the role I was portraying. "Did Rummy brush her teeth this morning?"*
>
> *I answered blankly, "I don't know."*
>
> *"Well, you'd better find out," he said.*
>
> *b.k.*

comfortable with the flow of the activity. After you stop the scene, you can discuss the "who" each student created. That's always interesting.

One important message for students to understand is this one:

Each character they create must be treated with respect. Each character must have dignity and dimension, just as real people do.

In other words, students should avoid easy stereotypes and clichés. They are trying to create "real" people, not cardboard cutouts.

A new place. Call out a new place and have students create new characters. A fruit stand or small market works well. Here are a few questions that will help draw out character details:

Who are you? Are you old or young? Do you move quickly or slowly? How is your eyesight? Have you had a good day or a bad day? Do you feel confident or shy and insecure? What are you doing in this place? Are you buying several items or a few? Do you have enough money to buy everything you want, or is money a problem? Are you open and friendly, or do you keep to yourself? Is there anyone here you know? Do you live in this town or are you visiting?

Then stop and discuss again, letting students describe their new personalities. Ask if the characters created were the same, different or similar to their real selves.

You might try . . . You might try having each student be responsible for a "Call a Place" round, selecting a place and calling out details and questions. A student thus assumes your role of side coach.

Another idea is to have students create a written version of "Call a Place." They have just brought a character to life by acting. Now ask them to bring the same character to life by writing. What does the character look like? What is the character doing in the designated place? How is the character feeling?

"Call a Place" leads quite easily and naturally into the next improvisation activity, "Three W's," page 64.

Three W's

"Three W's" is an improvisation that, for most teachers, never fails. It's a quick tune-in to the imagination, and people respond to it instantly, almost by reflex.

What are the Three W's? In this case they are **Who am I?**, **Where am I?**, and **What am I doing?**

The basics. For this activity, you will need a yardstick. (A three-foot dowel will also work.)

Hold up the yardstick and ask:

What is this?
A yardstick, the group will say.
What else?

It won't take students long to see that you are asking them to transform the object with their imaginations.

A pool cue, someone will shout.
A golf club.
A microphone.
A conductor's baton.
A baseball bat.
A blind person's walking stick.

Once students have warmed up to the idea, have each take out a piece of paper and write out one thing he thinks the yardstick could be — something other than what has already been mentioned by the class. Have the students fold their papers and put them in a hat.

Students then draw from the hat to find out what the yardstick is. Explain that they are to come forward and show — without speaking — who they are, where they are, and what they are doing, using the object as a prop.

Give students a few moments to plan, then have them begin their presentations. Here your energetic leadership is important:

*Okay, **who** is Kelly? . . . Yes, it appears she's being a female . . . a grown woman. **What** is she do-*

ing? Right. It seems she is talking on a cellular phone. How can you tell? Yes, she pulled that antenna out, and she looks like she's talking to someone. That was very clear. Do you think you can tell **where** she is? Kelly, give us an indication of where you might be talking on this cellular phone . . . Okay, it looks like she's in the car.

If the mood is friendly and open, you might add:

So, let's add another **W**. Show us **who** you're talking to, Kelly.

The actor adds a sigh.

She's talking to . . . who do you think? Yes, it might be her kids. She could be sighing with disgust at their bickering . . . or was that a lovesick sigh? We're going to have to see that again . . . Oh, now it's clear. That was definitely a lovesick sigh. She's talking to her boyfriend.

Side coaching is important with this activity (See page 16). Many students will draw slips with the same object, and they will have the same ideas for their presentation. That's all right. Say something like this:

If someone else does what you were going to do, do the same activity and add one thing, your own twist — a nod, a smile, a little something extra. For example, if you're a baseball player, maybe you can knock the dirt out of your cleats with the baseball bat before you hit the ball. Don't change your idea. Just add to it or give it something special.

The "Who am I?" part of each presentation usually needs an adjective for clarity. For example, if someone is a batter, say:

What kind of a batter are you? . . . I see. You're a **nervous** batter. Great.

If someone is a police officer, ask:

What kind of police officer are you? Show us . . . I'd say you are either an **angry** police officer or a **confident** police officer. I'm not sure. Show us a little more . . . Now it's clear. You are a very angry police officer.

I once did an intergenerational project with two drama groups —girls in a placement home for "neglected and delinquent juveniles" and elderly women in a troupe called "The Afterglow Players." The youngest actor in that troupe was 80 years old.

I adapted "Three W's" for teams of two. One team, a fifteen-year-old and an eighty-seven-year-old, transformed their yardstick into a rescue rope. The teenager clearly needed to be rescued from a ravine of some kind.

The woman dangled the yardstick-now-rope and hollered to the girl: "You'll be all right. I won't leave you, I promise. Just hold on. You don't know it, but I love you." When at last she pulled the girl out of the ravine, the two embraced. Through this simple activity, they had clearly made a real connection.

b.k.

To help students identify who they are, it is helpful to have a list of adjectives for them to choose from. You may want to photocopy the List of Adjectives in the Appendix (page 114).

Group presentations. You can also try "Three W's" as a group activity, with each group generating a 15-20 second "sound byte without the sound" that shows the transformed yardstick in action. For example, if the yardstick is a baseball bat, the group might show a pitcher, a batter and the umpire in a brief scenario. If the yardstick is a microphone, the group might show a singer, a drummer and a guitar player auditioning for a show.

You might try . . . You might try having students *write* a paragraph describing someone who is using the transformed yardstick. Again, remind them to be clear about who, what and where. Have students discuss the similarities between the information the actor must show and the information the writer must put on paper.

First Thing Said

With "First Thing Said," you give each group a sentence. That sentence must be used as the first sentence in a scene the group creates. The main rule is that *everyone* in a group has a role in both creating and performing the scene.

The basics. Divide your class into groups of four or five students each. Give each group a card with a sentence on it. Here are some sentences that work well for this activity:

- The rabid dog broke out of her cage.

- We'll never find our way back.

- Where's my oxygen mask?

- I smell smoke.

- I'm afraid of heights.

- The car won't start.

- Surprise!

- Looks like we'd better call 911.

- Get with it!

- I never thought I'd see you again.

- Promise you won't forget me.

- This is another fine mess you've gotten us into.

- That was my favorite one.

- The door won't open.

- That statue blinked!

- He won't hurt you.

- There — I've said it.

- The envelope, please.

- Keep digging — We're almost there.

- In this place, nothing would surprise me.

- Don't just stand there — Open it.

- They're gaining on us!

- Take it — I can't look at it any more.

Explain that each group is to create a short scene, using the sentence it has been given as the first thing said in the scene.

Emphasize the need to decide on a beginning, a middle and an end. Emphasize also that everyone in a group must have a role in the scene created.

Give groups a specific amount of time to plan their scenes — five minutes usually works well. Offer help if anyone needs it, and extend the time a bit if necessary.

Then have the groups present their scenes.

Machines

With "Machines," all participants get to exercise their imaginations while working together to create a human "machine." It is an excellent activity for teaching teamwork. If the machine isn't working, it's up to each group member to contribute some-thing to make it work.

Round one. Divide the class into several small groups of five to seven students each. Select one group to be the demonstration group.

Have one member of the demonstration group stand in the center of the room. Explain that the person is to choose a movement to repeat over and over. It should be a simple movement, nothing elaborate. The movement must be easy to repeat and to control, like raising an arm straight out to the side or kicking the left leg forward.

Continue:

Now we're going to build a machine. While Mike makes the movement he has chosen over and over, other members of his group will look to see where each of them can connect to his movement. Think quickly. Maybe one of you could be part of the mechanism that pulls the arm of the machine back and forth. Maybe someone could be part of the cooling system by rotating a hand above his head.

Mike, keep moving. Now, the rest of you, one at a time, go ahead and join Mike's machine.

When all members of the group have become part of the machine, give them more instructions:

Now we have a real machine here! Okay, ma-chine, speed up, up, up . . . Now slowwww dowwwwn . . . Slower, slower, slower . . . Now, slowly, increase to normal speed . . . You're up to speed . . . Now add a sound . . . That's it . . . Keep up that sound as you slowwww down again . . . and stop. Good job!

Next, let each small group create a machine before the class. Take each through the *speed up, slow down, return to normal, add a sound, slow to a stop* sequence.

Round two. Explain that you are going to whisper the name of a specific machine to each group. (Or, if you prefer, have the names of the machines written on index cards to hand out to each group.) The group then builds its designated machine. Some possible machines:

- motorcycle
- pinball machine
- typewriter
- music box
- television
- video game
- cuckoo clock
- washing machine

Give the groups a few minutes to get their machines up and running. Then have each group present its machine to the rest of the class.

Class members try to guess what machine is being presented. Warn about correct guesses that come too early:

Do what your group rehearsed. If someone guesses correctly, somehow let the group know that the person got it right. Then finish your presentation.

Round three. Explain to the students that they are to build a machine that does not exist yet. They are to invent it. Have them try the following machines:

- a good-bye machine
- a party machine
- a make-the-world-happy machine
- a frustration machine
- an encouragement machine

If no one is guessing correctly during the presentations, ask:

What is one thing you can do to make what you are doing more clear to everyone? Can you add something that will help us see and identify what you have built? Give it a try . . .

Challenge round. If there is time and interest, let students try coming up with both the idea for a kind of machine and the machine itself.

Two Storytellers

"Two Storytellers" is a group story telling activity that teaches active listening, improvisation, and an understanding of beginnings, middles and ends.

Warming up. Introduce storytelling by getting your group in a circle. Have a volunteer start a story and tell it for awhile. Then signal for that person to stop, and have someone else continue the story. (You might wander around the group and then tap someone's head to signal that the baton has been passed.)

This warm-up is harder than it seems. Students can't plan what they are going to say because they don't know what part of the story they will have to tell. It's important to do the warm up a number of times. It takes practice for students to learn that they need to relate to the ideas present in the story, instead of going off on some "Star Wars" tangent that doesn't have anything to do with what has gone before.

It is important to stress the idea of beginning, middle and end. If a warm-up story wanders all over the place, try leading a second round of the same activity and providing a structure:

The next story is about a group of neighborhood kids who form a baseball team. Although they aren't very good in the beginning, they work hard and win the city championship. Sydney, why don't you start the story . . .

Then, if the group starts wandering, you can re-mind them that they need to get this team to the playoffs.

When students have become comfortable with the warm-up, move on to the next level of story telling.

Writing. Ask students to write a very, very short story — no more than about three paragraphs long. The story should have a beginning, a middle and an end, just like the warm-up stories. The story should also include some specific characters and some specific actions that you will assign.

Using the List of Characters and the List of Actions from the Appendix (pages 105-116), choose several characters and several actions for the students to use in their first story. For example, you might require that the story involve a **bus driver**, a **clown**, a **tennis player**, a **scout leader** and an **astronaut**, as well as the actions of **clapping, robbing a bank, scratching** one's head, **looking closely at someone** and **hitting a ball with a bat.**

Emphasize that the students must find a way to combine these elements into a very short story with a beginning, a middle and an end.

Performing. Select two or three student stories to perform, and designate an area of the room as "The Space" (see page 15) for the performances.

Choose two students to come to The Space as storytellers. Give each student a copy of the first story. Explain that these two students will tell the story, one sentence at a time, alternating back and forth between them.

Next ask for volunteers to be the "players." Assign each player a number. (The first character to appear in the story is designated Player #1, the second as Player #2, etc.)

As the storytellers tell the story, the players listen for their characters to be identified. When the first character is mentioned in the story, Player #1 comes to The Space and performs whatever action is indicated by narration. When the second character is introduced, Player #2 comes forward and performs the action needed. Here's how it might begin:

*Storyteller #1: Once upon a time there was a **king** who was always **scratching** his head. In fact, he couldn't put his arm down at all because he was so busy **scratching.***

(Player #1 — the king — goes to The Space and pantomimes scratching his head.)

*Storyteller #2: Every morning, the **princess** would come into the room, **curtsey**, **pat her***

In one session of Two Story-tellers," two students named Laura and Judy were telling a story together, creating it as they went along. They introduced several characters, all of them active. Before I realized it, the whole class was in The Space.

Laura would notice if a particular character needed something new to do, and she would create it. Judy would have characters leave and bring in new characters.

The two made an excellent team. The story went on for several minutes, with everyone in the class engaged. I wanted to hire them as a full-time storytelling team!

b.k.

father gently on the back *and run off to* ***play jacks.***

(Player #2 — the princess— enters The Space, curtseys, pats the king on the back, and sits, pantomiming a game of jacks.)

Storyteller #1: **Three fiddlers** *came into the king's chambers every morning and* **played a fiddle** *tune. The* **King danced,** *but he couldn't put his arm down or stop scratching his head.*

(Three fiddlers enter The Space and pantomime playing a fiddle. The king dances while continuing to scratch his head . . . etc.)

Remind students of your guidelines for using appropriate language and gestures. You might also want to set up some movement boundaries. An example:

No one can shoot anyone and no one can fall down.

You might try . . . When your students seem ready for it, you might try moving from already-written stories to actual improvisation. Instead of reading a story, the storytellers create a story on the spot.

One storyteller starts the story and stops after 30 seconds or so. The second storyteller takes over and continues for approximately the same amount of time. The two storytellers thus "co-create" a story.

Emphasize that the storytellers should include many characters and a lot of action. As they mention the various characters, the players join the storytellers in The Space, performing the action suggested by the narration. For example, the storyteller might say:

. . . and the frog leaped up and stood in the corner shivering.

The designated player quickly goes to the Space, becomes a frog, and leaps and shivers.

The nearsighted Mr. McDuff shook the frog's hand.

The next player jumps up, becomes the near-sighted McDuff and shakes the frog's hand. Continue until the story reaches a natural conclusion. If it doesn't, you may need to side coach a comment like, "How does it end?" or "Then what?" or even "Okay, wrap it up now."

Visiting History

With "Visiting History," students look at an old object and imagine the story it might have to tell. A quilt works well, but you might also use an antique wheel, a beaded vest, an old hurricane lamp, a weathered box or any old object that might have an interesting history.

Looking at memories. Start by spending some time talking about memories. Ask students some questions about some of their own memories:

1. *What games do you remember from when you were a child? Where did you play them?*
2. *What was your group of friends like when you were small? What did you do together?*
3. *What do you remember from your very first days of school?*

Bring out an old patchwork quilt, preferably one that is old and worn, the more detailed, the better. (Or use any other old, interesting object.) Show the quilt to the students and invite them to gather around so they can see it and touch it.

Explain that the quilt contains many memories. The life of the quilt is a mystery that the students can unlock through the use of their imaginations.

Draw out ideas with the following questions:

1. *What can you tell about the quilt by feeling it? Smelling it? Looking at it?*

2. *When was this quilt made?*

3. *Was it made for some special occasion?*

4. *Who made it?*

5. *What were some of the happiest moments in the life of the quilt?*

6. *What was its narrowest escape?*

7. *Who loved it the most?*

8. *Was there anyone who wanted to throw it out or destroy it?*

9. *What was the quilt's greatest disappointment?*

10. *What was its best-kept secret?*

11. *What was the major turning point in its life?*

12. *How did the people who owned the quilt feel about each other? Did they treat the quilt with respect?*

Bringing memories to life. Divide the class into groups. Explain that each group will recreate a scene from the quilt's life.

Have students choose a scene idea, based on the previous discussion of the quilt's life. Then explain that they must address each of the following questions in creating their presentations:

1. *Where does the scene take place?*

2. *Who are the characters? What are their goals in the scene? How are they related?*

3. *What happens? Are there problems or obstacles? If so, how do the characters overcome them?*

There is often disagreement and discussion, so group members will have to make choices.

Have the groups rehearse their scenes and then present them for the class. Or make each scene an improvisation, letting the group members create the scene as they go.

You might try . . . Another idea is to plan a scene with the entire class. Then let different groups come forward and create different versions of the same scene.

Or you might divide the class into small groups and give each one a different object. Each group then creates a scene based on the life of that object.

You might also try having the class select scenes and put them all together into a complete drama of the quilt's life.

Freeze

"Freeze" is the basic of basics, the classic of classic improvisation games. It is also an activity that students always love.

A warning: Before you read the directions for this activity, move to a spot where there are no interruptions. Visualize each step as you read. While it may sound complicated on paper, the game — when it's up and running — actually moves fast and flows easily.

The basics. Ask for two volunteers to come forward or enter The Space. (See page 15.) Assign a simple situation for a scene — a ski lesson, for example.

The two volunteers begin acting out the scene. They continue until someone calls, "Freeze." Then they immediately freeze in position.

The person who called "Freeze" comes forward, taps one of the players, and assumes that player's position, literally. Whatever the person's body position, the new player mimics it exactly and then says something to initiate a completely new situation.

For example, if the replaced player happens to freeze in the position of bending over, ready to fall, the new player also assumes that position. Then the new player adds a statement like, "This is my first dance contest. It's tougher than I thought," thus setting up a new scene.

The two players continue that scene for awhile, until someone else calls "Freeze." Then a new player comes in, replacing one of the players and making a statement that sets up a new situation.

Remember. If students spend too much time with any one scene, that improvisation can become really, really laborious. Then the actors in the scene start getting negative feedback, and everyone has an unhappy experience. To prevent this, you may want to develop a twenty second limit to keep things rolling, especially at first. As soon as the actors have established the new situation and shown what the characters are doing, they don't need much more time. Someone needs to call "Freeze."

The most fun I have ever had with "Freeze" was when I was working with an enormous group of 95-100 high school students. I asked for four people at a time to be in a scene.

Whenever the scene became chaotic, I would call out, "Listen to each other. Keep it simple, pay attention to each other and tell the story clearly."

When everyone got the hang of it, the students created some impressive "mini stories" with their fast-acting imaginations.

b.k.

Improv Dialogues

Students can have a lot of fun creating scenes to go with the very short scripts that follow. You will be amazed at how they can use these odd little nonsense dialogues to come up with scenes that are perfectly logical.

You might want to warm up with a round of "Three W's" (page 64) before starting this activity.

The basics. Below are three very short scripts, with the characters in each scene defined only as "Character #1" and "Character #2." What students do is provide the context. Who are the people in the scene? Where are they? What are they doing?

Divide the class into groups of two, and assign a script to each group. Some groups will receive the same script, but that is part of the fun. The actors in each group establish who the characters are, where they are, and what they are doing. They must use only the words in their script and add nothing "outside of the lines."

Allow students two or three minutes to prepare and give the "within appropriate bounds" speech of your choice. (See "The A word," page 17.) Then have each group present its scene to the class.

You might try. . . Reproducing "List of Characters," "List of Actions," "List of Places" and "List of Situations" from the Appendix (pages 109-113) can be helpful. You might try letting students look at the lists for ideas.

You might also try grouping students into groups of four and trying the "Scripts for four"(pages 83-84.)

Scripts for two. Following are scripts for three short scenes for two people each (Scenes A-C):

Script A

(for two people)

Character #1: What are you doing here?

Character #2: I'd like to be able to tell you.

Character #1: Funny, our being here.

Character #2: Not very. I do peculiar things.

Character #1: But I've never known you to go this far.

Character #2: You mean because of the . . .

Character #1: Of course that's what I mean.

Character #2: It's just like me, though.

Character #1: That's true. Unbelievable, but true.

Script B

(for two people)

Character #1: Can it be?

Character #2: Maybe.

Character #1: It's not really obvious.

Character #2: But you can tell.

Character #1: I've never seen it before.

Character #2: I'm sure you've heard of it.

Character #1: Why would you think that?

Character #2: Isn't that what you've been telling everyone?

Character #1: Wow. No. Sorry if I gave you that impression.

Character #2: Well, it's too late now. Let's hope for the best.

My daughter Misha and I once teamed up for "Improv Dialogues" and performed Scenes A and B. In Scene A, she was Character #1, and I was Character #2. We were two skydivers; she was bold and I was petrified. We were in the plane, getting ready to make the jump.

In Scene B, we were a synchronized swimming team. She, Character #2, had changed the swim routine while we were in the middle of competition.

We tried to think of outlandish situations first and then see if we could make the dialogues fit. I think that approach is a good one for this activity.

b.k.

Script C

(for two people)

Character #1:   I wouldn't.

Character #2:   Think!

Character #1:   It would ruin everything.

Character #2:   Ruin what?

Character #1:   Everything . . . the way it is right now.

Character #2:   You can't really ruin it.

Character #1:   But this won't work.

Character #2:   You're right.

Character #1:   Well, let's flip a coin.

Character #2:   Give me a break.

Character #1:   Why? What's wrong?

Character #2:   I haven't got a coin.

Character #1:   Why didn't you say so? That solves everything.

Character #2:   You know something? You're right.

Scripts for four. On the next pages are two different scenes for four people each (Scenes D and E):

Script D

(for four people)

Character #1: We'd like to thank you for coming, and again — we are sorry.

Character #2: You were nice enough. Is this as far as it can go?

Character #3: Without creating a lot of trouble.

Character #4: We've gone to a lot of trouble already.

Character #1: We appreciate that, we really do. If it were possible, we would have never let this happen, but there's nothing we can do.

Character #2: Someone must. Who?

Character #3: It won't do much good.

Character #4: Let us find that out.

Character #1: There's no need to go through all of that . . . well, embarrassment.

Character #2: We're already very embarrassed.

Character #3: Look, why don't you just forget about it.

Character #4: I hope you can. We won't.

Script E

(for four people)

Character #1: No! I don't want you to do it! It's just not right. We haven't even talked it over. Let's at least do that much.

Character #2: You're obviously disturbed. We don't need to talk.

Character #3: You know, little by little, you're beginning to get on my nerves.

Character #4: Look, say what you want to say and then get out.

Character #1: You're acting crazy. That's what I want to say.

Character #2: Well, maybe there's something we can learn.

Character #3: Somebody had better learn something; I can tell you that.

Character #4: This can't go on.

Character #1: Exactly.

?
.

What Are You Doing?

For some reason, students of all ages feel comfortable with "What Are You Doing?" The results can be amazing, even in groups where self-esteem and confidence are not exactly skyrocketing. Groups just come alive.

The main thing to remember with "What Are You Doing?" is that people are pantomiming one action while they *say* they are doing something else. The activity really emphasizes thinking quickly and staying cool under pressure. Students also learn to laugh at themselves when they don't think quickly enough. That takes practice.

Back and forth. Have two people come forward to demonstrate the "back and forth" version of this game. The first person initiates an easy activity — jumping rope, for example. The second person asks, "What are you doing?"

The first person answers with a totally unrelated activity like, "I'm painting a fence." The second person begins to imitate painting a fence.

"What are you doing?" asks the first person. The second person answers with a totally unrelated activity like, "I'm eating an ice cream cone." The first person begins to imitate eating an ice cream cone.

The two continue, each imitating an action while *saying* that he or she is doing something else, until one person falters. Then someone else in class comes forward to replace that person.

Here's one more scenario, as an example:

Beth pantomimes putting gas in a car. David says, "What are you doing?"

Beth, while continuing to put gas in a car, says, "I'm petting my cat." David pantomimes petting a cat.

Beth says, "What are you doing?" David, while continuing to pet a cat, says, "I'm jumping on a trampoline." Beth pantomimes jumping on a trampoline.

Remind students that they can keep it simple. Answers like, "I'm working as a runway model" are clever and perfectly acceptable. However, simple answers like "I'm brushing my teeth" work just as well for the activity.

The "back and forth" version of this game requires a lot of concentration. Once students understand the basic concept from the demonstration, you might want to switch to the "in a line" version described below, which is actually easier and less threatening for many student but harder to explain. Later you can try coming back to the "back and forth" version.

In a line . . . The class is divided into two lines, Line A and Line B. The first person in Line A begins the action. The first person in Line B speaks:

Line B Person #1:   What are you doing?

Line A Person #1:   (Acting like a monkey in a zoo) I'm figure skating.

(Line B Person #1 starts pantomiming figure skating. Line A Person #1 goes to the end of the line. The next person in Line A then speaks.

Line A Person #2:   What are you doing?

Line B Person #1:   (Pantomiming figure skating) I'm putting on false eyelashes.

(Line B Person #1 then goes to the end of the line while Line A Person #2 pantomimes putting on false eyelashes. The next person in Line B then speaks.)

Line B Person #2:   What are you doing?

(The action continues, alternating between Line A and Line B.)

This version puts less pressure on students because each has to do only one action at a time, rather than a whole sequence of actions.

You might try . . . A nice twist to this activity is to require adding a compliment with each "What are you doing," especially if students often put each other down or exhibit unkind behaviors. The dialogue then sounds something like this:

Person #1:   *What are you doing?*

Person #2:   *(While pantomiming eating an ice cream cone) Knitting a sweater.*

Person #1:   *(As he begins knitting a sweater) Nice looking sweater.*

Taxi

"Taxi" is a fast-paced game where saying "yes" keeps the fun alive. The activity is often very funny, and students love it.

The basics. Create a taxi by arranging two chairs in front of the class or in The Space (See page 15). Ask one student to sit in the driver's seat and wait for someone to hail the cab.

A second student hails the cab, taking on a certain personality and setting the tone for the ride. If a very nervous person with a high-pitched voice hails the cab, the driver becomes nervous, with a high-pitched voice. If a very proper British tourist asks to go to the Lincoln Center, the taxi driver becomes a very proper British taxi driver discussing life in the city.

After the two students have had a brief "ride," another student steps forward and calls "Taxi!" That is the signal for the current driver to exit. The passenger scoots over and becomes the taxi driver, waiting to see who the passenger will be. If it's a Texas rodeo rider, the taxi driver becomes a Texan who loves the rodeo.

Always remind students that they don't have to do anything flashy or hilarious. That's not important. The important thing is to be clear. Both the driver and the passenger should try to stay in character.

You will also need to remind students that the driver takes on the traits of the passenger. If the passenger is a cheerful grandfather, the taxi driver can't decide to be a New York cab driver dealing with the grandfather. The driver must be a cheerful grandfather, too. Tell students:

Remember, match what the passenger gives you.

Real people vs. stereotypes. Comedy, drama, and improvisation are best when they present *real* people. Students need to be reminded that any time we "act as if" we are another person, we must respect that person. It's a good idea to discuss the concept of stereotypes and why we want to avoid them. While it's okay to exaggerate a situation for humor, students need to learn where the "line which we don't cross" is, and respect it.

You might try . . . To encourage all students to get involved, try assigning each a specific character to portray. You might get ideas from the "List of Characters" in the Appendix (page 109). Students still have to figure out what to say as the characters they have chosen, but they don't have to invent the characters as well.

Another idea is to give each student an adjective from the List of Adjectives (page 114) to combine with a character already chosen. For example, you might wind up with a *nervous* nurse or a *happy* electrician.

> *A group of eight teenagers in my "Teen Theatre" group played "Taxi" one day for about fifteen minutes. During that time, the actors were able to think of a variety of characters and never repeated types. No scene went on for more than 20 seconds before someone stepped forward and called "Taxi." At one point I looked over at the students who were observing the group. They were either standing or perched on the edge of their chairs, smiling.*
>
> *That kind of creative involvement is the goal of every improv game.*
>
> *b.k.*

Taking it further

Interested in taking active learning even further? This chapter will give you some ideas.

Where to Go from Here?

If you like active learning, you may want to go further with your students, trying activities and projects that are beyond the scope of this book. Here are just a few ideas to explore:

Volunteers. Bring volunteers and special guests into class to help make active learning come alive. (See "Working with Volunteers," page 94.)

Dramatic interpretation. Dramatic interpretation can be a memorable way to bring literature to life, as students present scenes from a novel or other literary work. They can dramatize a significant scene from the original work, or they can connect highlights of the work with original narration. (See "Dramatic Interpretation," page 96.)

Monologues. Have students write and present monologues on various topics. (See "Monologues," page 98.)

Role playing. Use role playing to help students resolve conflicts, solve problems or look for different solutions. (See "Role Playing," page 101.)

Interdisciplinary projects. Drama makes a perfect final outcome for an interdisciplinary project. For example, if students have been studying the colonial period of America through history, art, literature and music, the class might write and present an original script that helps demonstrate what life was like in that period of time.

A teen theater troupe. Perhaps the ultimate in active learning is the creation of a teen theater troupe. Teen theater involves young people presenting original scripts about issues they care about. (See "Teen Theater," page 103.)

Working with Volunteers

The notion that "it takes an entire village to *raise* a child" is certainly true of *educating* a child. In a one-teacher classroom, volunteers and guests can help breathe life into learning.

Consider reaching out to expand the benefits of drama in your classroom. There are many people who might be happy to come in and work with your students. Just a few ideas: Students from the drama class at a local high school, drama students from a nearby community college or university, the director of a local community theater production and actors from the community.

The initial effort to bring volunteers into your classroom may take a little time; but the payoff is well worth it. Here are a few guidelines for working successfully with volunteers:

- Think specifically. What would you like your guest to contribute? You might want to brainstorm ideas with potential volunteers, perhaps even involving students as well.

- Ask for an "asker." Some parent volunteers are willing to invest time setting up a network of reliable guests. Take time to meet with the "asker" and chat about ideas and expectations.

- Value spontaneous opportunities. Is there a troupe of Russian actors in town? See if your classroom can host a meeting with the actors, who can probably be coaxed into a small performance. Did your friend who teaches at the community college just tell you about a presentation given by a student who is a marvelous mime artist? Holler "Encore!" and invite that student to your classroom.

- Deal with details. When you are lucky enough to have high-quality performers and presenters in your classroom, you want the experience to be rich for everyone. Think of all of the variables that might interfere with the presentation, and deal with them ahead of time.

   If a mime student visits your class, for example, does she plan to involve the class in a mime activity? Perhaps your "asker" could find someone to come to the classroom that day to help with one of the groups. Ask if the mime artist has some associates who might come for an hour and participate with your students. Find a way to create enough structure so that your students can stay focused and succeed in the planned activity.

- Expand your Rolodex. Check out your local arts council. The artists there will often be available for one-day to six-week residencies. Cultivate grant writers who can help you raise funds to pay for a residency. Come up with a great idea and ask an artist to help you make it happen. Ask if anybody else has a great idea, and ask an artist to help you make it happen. Ask for a great idea from an artist, and make it happen together.

The Carnegie Council on Adolescent Development's Task Force on Education of Young Adolescents made eight recommendations for middle schools in its 1989 report, *Turning Points: Preparing American Youth for the 21st Century* (The Carnegie Council on Adolescent Development, Washington, D.C., 1989). It called for creating "communities for learning where close, mutually respectful relationships with adults and peers are considered fundamental for intellectual development and personal growth." One way to encourage such relationships is by bringing qualified guests into your classroom to help with active learning. Then important mentorship relationships can occur naturally.

Mentorships are an important way to see how subjects we learn about in school work in the real world.

I have served as a volunteer mentor to a number of students who are interested in pursuing a career in theater arts. One young woman did a "job shadowing" with me for a day to fulfill an assignment in her "Careers" class.

She asked, "What do you like best about your job?"

I told her, "I do the work I love and get paid for it."

*She smiled. "I notice you didn't say you get paid **a lot**!"*

b.k.

Dramatic Interpretation

One way of linking drama to what your class is studying is with cuttings from a work of literature. "Highlights," below, describes one approach that can be varied in many ways.

Highlights. Divide the class into teams of at least two students each. Explain that students are to select a highlight from the novel (or short story) you are studying in class, turning the scene from literature into a short play to present to the class. Explain:

In selecting a portion of the book for your play, choose a scene that reveals something important about the characters, plot or theme of the book. Choose a scene with interesting dialogue and, ideally, some action.

Drop any "tags" in the book — in other words, the "he saids" and "she saids." If a scene is very long, you may want to cut some dialogue. Otherwise, leave the dialogue just the way it is.

How will you "stage" your scene? Plan ahead and rehearse your presentation.

An example of a highlight that might be dramatized is the scene from *To Kill a Mockingbird* where Atticus questions Mayella Ewell, witness for the prosecution.

Variations. There are many ways to give more specific and challenging criteria for "Highlights." For example, you might assign each team a different character from the book. Then ask each team to choose a scene that especially illustrates its character's traits.

Another variation is to ask students to find every line spoken about a specific topic. For example, they might look for every line spoken about the horse in Steinbeck's *The Red Pony.* How do the characters' relationships with the horse differ? Teams combine all of these lines into a series of cuttings from the book, perhaps connecting them all with dialogue by a narrator.

Steinbeck's book, *The Pearl,* shows characters in relationship to the pearl that is central to the story. You might ask students to arrange, connect and present (with appropriate attitude and inflection) each character's statements about the pearl. It's amazing the impact that this type of "lifting from text" can have.

Over the years, I have developed approximately 60 "highlights" scripts for a workshop called "Briskworks." These scripts are cuttings from literature, centered around a theme. Some favorites include "Family," "Friends in Fantasy," "The Greeks" and "Frontiers."

The cuttings are about five minutes long and are joined together with transitional dialogue to form a seamless script. My students memorize their lines for the program, which they present wearing costumes of T-shirts with our Briskworks logo.

Highlights scripts provide a low-cost theater of the imagination, accomplished in a short time and with a minimum of costuming, props and scenery.

b.k.

Monologues

Many people today share a stereotype about young people: "They are so self-centered and apathetic. They just don't **care** about anything."

"Individual care-abouts" gives students a chance to disprove this notion. The final project in this activity is the creation and presentation of student monologues.

Individual care abouts. Talk with students about stereotypes that exist about young people today. You will probably get a list that includes stereotypes like, "They're all gang members" or, "They all ride skateboards and wear weird clothes," or, "They're so materialistic."

If they don't bring it up themselves, ask students if they have heard, "They just don't **care** about anything." They will have. Ask:

So is it true that you don't care about anything?

A few will jokingly say "yes," but at least some students will admit there are people and things they care about.

Ask students what *they* care about.

After discussion, have students each write one sentence that describes something they care about. The subjects might be drawn from general categories like personal relationships, world issues, plans for the future, hobbies or personal interests. After they write their sentences, have them fold their papers once and put them in a hat passed around the room.

Mix up the papers in the hat. Then ask each student to draw a slip and read what is on it. The result is likely to be a wide variety of "care-abouts" from the group — certainly not what the stereotype suggests. Have someone make a list of all the topics mentioned.

Creating monologues. With students, look at the list of "care abouts" that they have created. Ask them to choose one of the issues to focus on, or to choose another issue:

Whatever topic you choose, answer these questions:

1. *Does this issue represent a large problem in the world?*

2. *Does it hit fairly close to home? If so how?*

3. *If you could change one thing about it right now, what would it be?*

Explain that these questions will help students in preparing the next part of this assignment, which is a monologue:

A monologue is your personal statement about the issue you care about. It is just you talking.

*However, a monologue is still a dramatic presentation. That means you can decide who you are. You can be you, or you can be someone else. You can also decide who you are talking **to** in the monologue.*

In a way, a monologue is like a story because you tell it to others. It must be clear; it must contain a beginning, a middle and an end. Make it short, about a minute and a half.

You might use humor if you want, or you might use a story from your own life experience to really make it clear to us why this issue is important to you. If you need to quote facts, please be accurate. This might mean a trip to the library, of course.

Giving students time in class to complete this activity makes you available as a resource to discuss possible topics and to help students create their two or three paragraph monologues. Giving them a class period to do the first draft and another to polish it will let them know that you are expecting a "beyond the obvious" look at the issue.

It's a good idea to let students share the first draft in a small group of four or five of their peers. Perhaps the members of the group can offer each other ideas for improvement. Then each person prepares the final draft of the monologue.

One year a member of my Stand Tall teen theater troupe experienced the death of her 20-year-old brother. She was devastated by the loss. When the troupe members discussed possible subjects for the monologues they would perform that season, the girl decided to write a monologue about how she was dealing with her grief.

The monologue was very powerful, describing the challenges she faced, her search for a reason to go on and her struggles to find the courage to fight, no matter how hopeless life seemed at times.

At nearly every performance that season, the actor was surrounded by girls from the audience who wanted to tell her that they understood, that they too had experienced losses — grandmothers, grandfathers, sisters, mothers. Some of the girls just wanted to thank her for sharing something so authentic and heartfelt. Her monologue had a tremendous impact.

b.k.

As students listen to each other's monologues, they will probably want to discuss the ideas presented. Many will share similar thoughts and experiences.

You might try . . . If you are pleased with your students' monologues, you might have the group share their ideas further in a performance. Connect the monologues with a short, unifying introduction and a thought-provoking concluding statement. This can be a great start if you decide to really "go for it" and create a teen theater troupe. (See page 103.)

Role Playing

Role playing can be a very effective technique for helping students to solve problems or resolve conflict. "Rewind — Friends" helps students look at problems by role-playing situations and then "rewinding and replaying" the scenes in various ways.

"Rewind — friends" gives students an opportunity to develop alternatives to ineffective communication patterns, beginning with their friends.

Rewind — friends. Start by asking students, "What is the most important thing to you in a friend?" Responses usually include "honesty," "loyalty," "trust," "someone I can be comfortable with," "someone who doesn't tell my secrets," "someone who likes me the way I am." Then ask:

What happens when your friendship hits a rough spot?

Conflict is a very natural aspect of any relationship. However, there are ways to learn to resolve or at least manage conflict when it occurs.

When we do have conflict, our goal is to reach a solution, not to gain a victory. Since our friends are important to us, we want to listen and make a real effort to understand.

Role playing. Prepare ahead of time a list of situations that involve conflict between friends. Divide the class into teams of two or three, and give each team a situation.

Here are a few situations that work well:

- You come in late to the lunchroom. People sitting at a table together reject you.

- You discover a note one of your friends wrote to another friend. It says mean things about you.

- You find out that someone — not your best friend, but someone you have always thought was okay — has been hassling your little brother.

101

- Someone you like very much has been avoiding you.

- Your best friend has been telling you incredible lies.

- You discover that a friend who has visited your house has taken something that belongs to you

- A friend has claimed credit for something you did.

- A friend has been bossing you around and not listening to what you have to say.

- You think your friend has changed.

- Your feelings have changed for your friend.

- It seems to you that your friend is always whining or complaining.

Ask each team to create a clear picture of its scene. Explain:

Just show us the problem that can arise between friends. Don't resolve it; just show us the problem.

Three to five minutes will probably be enough time for teams to develop their ideas and assign roles. If not, adjust to meet your group's needs. Have each team present its scene. After the scene, discuss the problem presented with the class. What ideas do students have for resolving the conflict?

Have the team "rewind" the scene and present it again, this time showing a way to resolve the problem. Discuss the resolution. Students may want to replay the scene with different endings, discussing the effectiveness of each resolution.

Resolutions are not always neat and tidy. You might want to address that fact, perhaps saying something like this:

Nick came into this scene feeling bad about his friendship with Matt, and I can see why. So, is there an easy way out of this one? . . . . . What's the best he can do in this situation?

This line of questioning leads away from simplistic solutions.

Teen Theater

Teen theater can have a powerful impact, both on the teens who perform and on the audiences who hear what they have to say. For those interested in the possibility of forming a teen theater group, I have described below the teen theater groups that I direct.

bobbi kidder

Alive Together!* and *Stand Tall. I started a teen theater troupe in my community eight years ago. I had seen Family Life Theatre in New York and New Image in San Diego and was impressed by the power of teens talking to teens. I decided to work with local teens to develop a model that would work for us.

That has led to the formation of two troupes in my community. *Alive Together!* includes both young men and young women, and *Stand Tall* includes only young women. Both groups perform for schools, community groups and churches throughout Oregon. *Stand Tall's* target audience is fifth through seventh grade girls, and its primary purpose is to promote courage and confidence among young girls.

We create our own material for the performances — scenes and monologues that explore the issues the troupes identify as having the greatest impact in their lives. The purpose is to show others what teenagers are thinking about and to stimulate discussion. Issues might include family communication, alternatives to violence and saving the environment, for example.

Students from all five community high schools audition in the spring for the troupes. Only eight individuals are selected for each troupe, and all of the performers are juniors and seniors. Each troupe is together for one year, and sometimes individuals will stay on for another year, providing leadership to newcomers.

We rehearse once a week for two hours, and I try to schedule performances so that the troupe members don't miss too much school. In general, this has worked well. In some cases, I have to remind actors that it is their responsibility to inform teachers of the troupe's performance schedule.

Parents have been very supportive, and I get positive feedback about the skills the young people learn in a season: the ability to be flexible, to work in a team, to be spontaneous, and to perform for a variety of audiences.

Suggestions. For people interested in starting a teen theater troupe, I have several suggestions that have worked for me.

One is to develop a contract for all participants. The contract makes very clear the expectations for troupe members about commitment and reliability. I have included a copy of the contract I use for *Stand Tall* and *Alive Together!* (See Appendix, pages 115-116.)

Another suggestion is to set guidelines, before you ever meet with students, about your goals as director and how far you want to go with issues. Some subjects may not "play well" in your community, although they would be just fine in the community down the road. You, as director, need to set guidelines for public performances with your troupe.

It is very helpful to schedule an overnight retreat to begin the season. The retreat helps students get to know one another. They also develop a sense of being a team as they work together to accomplish concrete goals like shopping together and preparing meals. At the retreats for each of my groups, we also go over the contract for members and develop a mission statement for the troupe.

An advisory board of community leaders can also provide vital support in keeping a troupe running. The six board members for *Alive Together!* and *Stand Tall* help us with fund raising and publicity for our public performances.

Directing a teen theater troupe is a big commitment. Juggling schedules can be a headache, and the actors' personal problems can be a heartbreak. However, each year I renew my commitment gladly and always enjoy the rewards immensely.

Appendix

The following information can be used with a variety of activities in *ImaginACTION*. The material on these pages is reproducible for the purchaser's own personal use in the classroom.

Verb Bank

Accelerate	Collapse	Fizz	Inflate	Ooze
Aim	Contract	Fizzle	Jab	Open
Amble	Crack	Flap	Jam	Overturn
Anchor	Cradle	Flee	Jerk	Pat
Angle	Crash	Flick	Jig	Patter
Approach	Crawl	Flinch	Jiggle	Pause
Arch	Creep	Fling	Jog	Peddle
Ascend	Cringe	Flip	Join	Peel
Babble	Crinkle	Float	Jostle	Perch
Balance	Crouch	Flop	Jump	Pile
Beep	Crumble	Flow	Kick	Pivot
Bend	Crumple	Flutter	Kneel	Plod
Billow	Crunch	Fly	Knock	Plop
Bob	Crush	Fold	Launch	Plow
Bounce	Curl	Freeze	Lean	Plug
Bound	Dance	Gallop	Leap	Plunge
Bow	Dart	Glide	Lie	Plunk
Break	Dash	Glower	Lift	Point
Brush	Dig	Grab	Limp	Polish
Bubble	Dip	Grasp	Litter	Polka
Bump	Dive	Grind	Lower	Pop
Burst	Dodge	Grip	Lunge	Pounce
Carry	Drag	Grow	Lurch	Pound
Carve	Draw	Gyrate	March	Prance
Catch	Drift	Hang	Mash	Press
Chat	Drip	Hit	Meander	Prowl
Cheer	Drive	Hobble	Meet	Pucker
Chew	Droop	Hold	Melt	Pull
Chop	Drop	Hop	Mince	Punch
Circle	Elevate	Hover	Nail	Push
Clasp	Enclose	Hug	Nap	Quake
Climb	Entwine	Hunt	Narrow	Quiver
Close	Erupt	Hurl	Nibble	Race
Clutch	Expand	Hustle	Nod	Ram
Coil	Explode	Infiltrate	Nudge	Rap

Verb Bank

(continued)

Recoil	Shrivel	Squash	Swish	Vacillate
Release	Shudder	Squeeze	Swivel	Vault
Revolve	Shuffle	Squirm	Swoop	Veer
Ripple	Shut	Squirt	Tackle	Ventilate
Rise	Sidle	Stack	Tap	Vibrate
Rock	Sing	Stagger	Tear	Waddle
Roll	Sink	Stalk	Tense	Walk
Rotate	Sip	Stamp	Throw	Wallow
Rub	Sit	Stand	Tickle	Waltz
Run	Sizzle	Step	Tie	Wander
Rush	Skate	Stick	Tilt	Wave
Sail	Ski	Stir	Tip	Weave
Sand	Skid	Stoop	Tiptoe	Whip
Saunter	Skip	Straighten	Topple	Whirl
Saw	Slice	Stretch	Toss	Wiggle
Scamper	Slide	Stride	Totter	Wilt
Scatter	Slink	Stroke	Touch	Wind
Scoop	Slip	Stroll	Tramp	Wink
Scramble	Slither	Strut	Trap	Wither
Scratch	Slouch	Stuck	Tremble	Wobble
Scrub	Soak	Stuff	Trim	Wrestle
Scurry	Soar	Surround	Trip	Wriggle
Settle	Spill	Suspend	Trudge	Wring
Sew	Spin	Swarm	Tug	Wrinkle
Shake	Spiral	Swat	Turn	Writhe
Shatter	Splash	Sway	Twirl	Yammer
Shave	Spray	Sweep	Twist	Yank
Shiver	Spread	Swerve	Two step	Yawn
Shoot	Spring	Swim	Type	Zigzag
Shop	Sprinkle	Swing	Uncurl	Zip
Shrink	Spurt	Swirl	Unite	Zoom

List of Characters

- actor
- ambulance driver
- archeologist
- army sergeant
- astronaut
- athletic coach
- auctioneer
- auto mechanic
- baby-sitter
- baker
- ballet dancer
- band director
- bank teller
- barber
- baseball player
- basketball player
- boxer
- brain surgeon
- bull fighter
- bus driver
- carnival worker
- carpenter
- cartoon character
- caveman/woman
- clown
- comedian
- computer operator
- concert pianist
- construction worker

- cook
- cowhand
- dancer
- dentist
- detective
- doctor
- famous inventor
- farmer
- father
- film maker
- fire fighter
- flight attendant
- disk jockey
- football player
- forest ranger
- fortune teller
- garbage collector
- grandfather
- grandmother
- grocery clerk
- gym teacher
- hermit
- home ec teacher
- hunter
- ice skater
- janitor
- jeweler
- jockey
- jogger
- judge
- karate expert
- king

- landlord
- lawyer
- lifeguard
- magician
- mail carrier
- jury member
- millionaire
- model
- mother
- movie star
- nurse
- Olympic swimmer
- painter
- photographer
- pilot
- pioneer
- pizza maker
- plumber
- poker player
- police officer
- political candidate
- President of USA
- prince
- princess
- principal
- prisoner
- queen
- race car driver
- receptionist
- robot

- rock singer
- sailor
- salesperson
- Santa Claus
- scientist
- sculptor
- shepherd
- ski instructor
- skydiver
- skyjacker
- soldier
- someone's pet
- spy
- stock broker
- street cleaner
- tailor/seamstress
- taxi driver
- teacher
- telephone operator
- tennis player
- tour guide
- tourist
- toy maker
- truck driver
- waitress/waiter
- weather reporter
- wild animal
- worker on strike
- World War I aviator
- writer

List of Actions

- adding spices to spaghetti sauce
- addressing a jury while defending a client in court
- admiring yourself in front of a mirror
- answering the phone
- apologizing
- asking for a raise
- backing out of a driveway
- baking cookies
- begging
- blowing up a balloon
- bowling
- braiding your hair
- buckling a belt
- building something with Legos
- burning your finger on the stove
- burping a baby
- buttoning a shirt
- buying groceries
- calling someone to ask for a date
- carrying a very heavy box
- catching a hat that's blowing down the street
- catching a pass

- changing a tire
- checking out a library book
- chewing bubble gum
- clapping
- climbing a mountain
- climbing a tree
- congratulating a friend
- crying
- cutting meat for a child
- dancing
- depositing a check
- driving bumper cars
- eating a candy bar
- eating a lemon
- eating a Popsicle
- eating an ice cream cone on a hot day
- eating chips and salsa, dripping salsa on your shirt
- eating food
- eating pizza
- eating spaghetti
- eating with chopsticks
- emptying garbage
- feeding the cat
- filling a car with gas
- finding out you have won the lottery

- flirting
- flying an airplane
- folding a flag
- following someone, trying to remain unseen
- getting gum off the bottom of your shoe
- getting the mail
- hanging a picture
- helping a small child stand and walk
- hitting a ball with a bat
- hitting your thumb with a hammer
- holding a snake
- holding a squirming baby
- ironing
- jogging
- learning to tap dance and not finding it easy to do
- lifting weights
- lighting a match
- loading the dishwasher
- looking closely at someone
- losing a helium-filled balloon
- making a free-throw
- making a milk shake

List of Actions

(continued)

- making a phone call in a phone booth
- making coffee
- mowing the lawn
- painting a room
- petting a dog
- picking out a video to rent
- pitching a baseball
- playing a fiddle
- playing an accordion
- playing cards
- playing darts
- playing Frisbee with a dog
- playing jacks
- playing miniature golf
- playing with a kitten and a ball of yarn
- polishing toenails
- putting on lipstick
- putting on mascara
- putting out a fire
- rafting
- walking on tiptoes so no ones hears you
- reading a magazine
- reeling in a big fish

- riding a bicycle
- riding an elevator
- robbing a bank
- Rollerblading
- saddling a horse
- sanding a table top
- scratching
- sewing on a button
- sewing with a sewing machine
- singing a song
- skiing
- skipping
- slamming your finger in the car door
- slipping on a banana peel
- smelling rotten eggs
- standing to give a speech and finding you've lost your notes
- swatting a fly
- swimming
- swinging on a tire swing
- taking a photograph
- taking a test
- taking someone's order at a restaurant
- throwing a pass

- throwing a temper tantrum
- trying on earrings
- trying to be nice after tasting something horrible
- trying to get away from a bee
- trying to keep from sneezing
- trying to open a broken umbrella as the rain starts
- trying to pick up a piece of paper on a windy day
- trying to take a nap but being annoyed by a buzzing fly
- trying to zip up a pair of tight jeans
- tying a shoe
- using a hula hoop
- walking a very big dog on a short leash
- walking barefoot on hot sand
- washing the car
- watching a movie, behind a tall guy
- watching a tennis match
- wrapping a present

List of Places

- airplane
- airport
- alley
- art gallery
- attic
- backstage
- bakery
- barn
- baseball field
- basement
- beach
- beauty salon
- bus station
- carnival
- castle
- cemetery
- circus
- city hall
- classroom
- concert
- day care center
- dentist's office
- desert
- doctor's waiting room
- dog show
- driving school
- elevator

- emergency room
- farm
- flea market
- forest
- garage
- grocery store
- gum factory
- gym
- haunted house
- health food store
- hospital
- hotel lobby
- hotel room
- ice skating rink
- inside a cannon
- inside a video game
- jungle
- kitchen
- Laundromat
- library
- marketplace
- moon
- mountain top
- movie theater
- museum
- on a roller coaster
- prison

- palace
- park
- pet shop
- police station
- post office
- race track
- radio/TV station
- restaurant
- retirement home
- rock concert
- rodeo
- roof top
- ship
- sidewalk
- Starship Enterprise
- subway station
- supermarket
- swimming pool
- the opera
- time machine
- toy factory
- tree house
- under a thumbnail
- wagon train
- wax museum
- White House
- zoo

List of Situations

- A brand new teacher tries to discipline a dramatically emotional student.

- A child gets an active puppy as a gift.

- A coach tries to inspire a lazy athlete.

- A film director is working with inexperienced actors.

- A group discovers that the "Honey, I Shrunk the Kids" guy has shrunk them, too.

- A mail carrier gets caught reading someone else's mail.

- A new servant starts to sit down and eat with the very proper master or mistress of the mansion.

- A parent tries to get a child to eat just one bite of peas.

- A person who is very thrifty and careful is buying a used car from an aggressive salesperson.

- A shy person tries to sell cookies to a hurried, busy person.

- A speeder tries to talk a police officer out of a ticket.

- A TV news reporter is trying to get an interview with a big star.

- After several tries, a frustrated customer gets the wait person's attention.

- An angry customer tries to return a defective product to a sales clerk trying to talk on the phone to a friend.

- An old boyfriend shows up at his ex-girlfriend's wedding.

- Athletes in a locker room bemoan the loss of the "big game."

- Firefighters respond to a four-alarm fire.

- On a plane, a talkative person sits next to someone who just wants to read.

- One person is about ready to bite into a donut or a slice of pizza that the other person wants.

- One person talks another out of jumping off a ledge.

- Students are cheating on a test.

- Three children home alone watch a horror movie.

- Three friends meet at a men's club where no women are allowed. Character #3 is a woman.

- Tourists arrive at a hotel which has lost their reservations.

- Two adversaries prepare to run the big race.

- Two hearty mountaineers are lost in the forest.

- Two people discover they have no money or credit cards when the check comes for an expensive dinner.

- Two people discuss the possibility of breaking out of jail.

- Two people fight over the TV remote control.

- Two people who used to know each other meet again while one is robbing the other.

List of Adjectives

- adventurous
- agitated
- angry
- antagonistic
- athletic
- bemused
- boisterous
- boorish
- bouncy
- brilliant
- brooding
- combative
- confident
- cool
- courageous
- creepy
- cynical
- desperate
- direct
- drab
- dramatic
- drowsy
- dynamic
- easygoing
- energetic
- excited
- expressionless

- exuberant
- flamboyant
- formal
- friendly
- frightened
- generous
- glowing
- goofy
- grasping
- happy
- hard-boiled
- hostile
- impersonal
- jolly
- lifeless
- lively
- lonely
- mean
- meddlesome
- mellow
- miserable
- mushy
- negative
- nervous
- orderly
- overbearing
- patient

- peculiar
- persistent
- petulant
- philanthropic
- phony
- practical
- quiet
- relaxed
- reserved
- scatterbrained
- secretive
- shy
- skeptical
- skittish
- surprised
- suspicious
- sweet
- tense
- timid
- traditional
- traitorous
- trustworthy
- unskilled
- vocal
- witty
- youthful
- zany

Sample Contract

for Teen Theater Troupe Members

Before I signed his document, I read and understood the points listed below. My signature indicates my acceptance of the conditions of this contract.

1. I know that I am part of an ensemble, a theater troupe.

    - My participation is essential to our success. (Success here is defined as "Building a program which has a significant impact on our community.")

    - Rehearsals and performances are essential to our success.

    - My participation means that I will attend rehearsals and performances.

2. This teen theater group is a priority for me. I know I will have to communicate with my teachers, employers and my family in order to enhance the image of the group as a professional theater ensemble and to make it easier on myself.

    - I will consider the people in my life who might benefit from schedule details and/or invitations to performances.

    - I will speak to each one of these people about my commitment to the theater troupe, show them the existing schedule and discuss time management issues which arise.

    - If I need to discuss any schedule conflicts with the theater troupe, I will do so in a timely manner. I will do this before missing a rehearsal or performance. In case of emergency, I will notify the director by telephone if I will not be at a rehearsal or performance.

3. I know that when my behavior in rehearsals, performances and in my daily life is focused on success, I feel stronger and more capable, like I'm doing my job well. (Success here is defined as "Living life committed to your personal best.")

    - I will come to rehearsals alert and ready to work.

    - If I make a commitment to write a script or schedule a performance, I will follow through.

    - I will support others in our ensemble by offering positive feedback and communicating honestly when problems arise.

    - I will listen to ideas and pay attention to suggestions.

    - I will participate appropriately in discussions.

4. I expect to meet my expectations for success in this theater group. (Success here is a combination of the first two definitions: Living my life committed to my personal best

and working to build in our teen theater program a program that will have a significant impact in the community.) I understand that I will support others and ask for their support in meeting these expectations.

5. I know that there is a slim-to-none chance that I will fall short of reaching my expectations for success in this teen theater group. If that happens, I know that we will discuss this contract and make a decision about my future involvement with the troupe.

   - I know, for example, that this discussion will happen if I miss one rehearsal or performance without advance or emergency notification.

   - I know that it is likely that after two such lapses, I will be given a brief farewell party.

   - I know that although absences discussed in advance are helpful, my participation is more helpful. So, legitimate reasons for absence from rehearsal or performance will also be reviewed.

Signature of the teen theater troupe member: _____

Signature of the teen theater troupe director: _____

Date: _____

About bobbi kidder

Author bobbi kidder teaches theater arts and interpersonal communication at Rogue Community College in Grants Pass, Oregon. She also directs teen theater troupes called *Stand Tall* and *Alive Together!*

Throughout her career, she has conducted drama workshops with a wide variety of groups in community centers, churches, classrooms, psychiatric hospitals, businesses, treatment centers, refugee camps and migrant education programs. Participants have ranged from ages 4 to 95 and have included groups in three foreign countries.

One of her favorite scenes in a movie is the barn-raising scene in the film *Witness*. "It is symbolic," she says, "of what I love best about life — people working together, enjoying the experience and getting the job done."

More books for teachers

from Cottonwood Press

Homework's Not Another Word for Something Else to Lose —
Helping Students WANT to Succeed in School and Then Setting Them Up for Success $19.95

ImaginACTION —
Using Drama in the Classroom, No Matter What You Teach $14.95

Hot Fudge Monday —
Tasty Ways to Teach Parts of Speech to Students Who Have a Hard Time
Swallowing Anything to Do with Grammar $18.95

Ideas that Really Work! —
Activities for English and Language Arts $21.95

Journal Jumpstarts —
Quick Topics and Tips for Journal Writing $5.95

Writing Your Life —
Autobiographical Writing Activites for Young People $14.95

My Personal Yearbook —
A Student's Own Unique, Personal Book of Memories $6.95

Row, Row, Row Your Class —
Using Music as a Springboard for Writing, Exploration and Learning $12.95

When They Think They Have Nothing to Write About —
The Cottonwood Composition Book.. $14.95

Games for English and Language Arts —
Reproducible Games that Challenge Students $16.95

Surviving Last Period on Fridays and Other Desperate Situations —
The Cottonwood Game Book $14.95

Mystery of the Suffocated Seventh Grader —
A Play to Read Aloud in Class.. $8.95

If They're Laughing, They're Not Killing Each Other —
Ideas for Using Humor Effectively in the Classroom, Even If You're Not Funny Yourself........... $12.95

Hide Your Ex-Lax Under the Wheaties —
Poems about Schools, Teachers, Kids and Education... $5.95

and more!

To order more copies of *ImaginACTION* . . .

Please send me _____ copies of *ImaginACTION*. I have enclosed $14.95 for each book ordered, plus 10% shipping and handling. (Colorado residents please add 3% sales tax.)

Please check one:

❏ Home   ❏ School

Name _____

(School) _____

Address _____

City_____ State_____ Zip _____

Method of Payment:

❏ Check   ❏ VISA   ❏ MasterCard   ❏ Purchase Order
                                                          (Please attach)

Credit Card # _____ Exp. Date _____

Signature_____

(Please make checks payable to Cottonwood Press, Inc.)

MAIL!

Cottonwood Press, Inc.
305 West Magnolia, Suite 398
Fort Collins, CO 80521

PHONE!

Order quickly by phone with
VISA or MasterCard
1-800-864-4297